A TOOL KIT FOR PROMOTING GENDER EQUALITY IN PUBLIC–PRIVATE PARTNERSHIPS

NOVEMBER 2023

ASIAN DEVELOPMENT BANK

CONTENTS

TABLES, FIGURES, AND BOXES

TABLES

FIGURES

BOXES

FOREWORD

Gender equality and women's empowerment are high on the world's development agenda and are recognized globally as driving forces for inclusive growth and development, and as a critical aspect in reducing poverty. Despite significant progress, gender inequality persists in Asia and the Pacific across multiple areas, including employment and economic opportunities; access to services, resources, and technologies; and leadership and decision-making. These inequalities have only been worsened by the negative consequences of the coronavirus disease (COVID-19) pandemic. The World Economic Forum's Global Gender Gap Report 2021 noted that, as a result of the impact of the pandemic, the estimated period of time required to close the global gender gap has been extended from 99.5 years pre-pandemic to 135.6 years post-pandemic.

Urgent action is required, and both the public and the private sectors can play an important role in reducing gender inequalities and opening opportunities for more inclusive development. To this end, public–private partnership (PPP) has the potential to play a catalytic role to connect public and the private actors and amplify the impact of gender actions that each sector undertakes.

The Asian Development Bank (ADB) has a strong commitment and focus on gender equality across its operations in both the public and the private sectors. "Accelerating progress in gender equality" is one of the seven operational priorities of ADB's Strategy 2030. As such, ADB assists both the public and the private sectors in the identification, conceptualization, structuring, preparation, and implementation of infrastructure projects. This support encompasses several areas, including developing an enabling environment and PPP frameworks for private sector engagement, building the capacity of government institutions and officials, and facilitating the development of essential and fundamental infrastructure required for economic activities. Integrating a gender perspective in PPP legal and institutional frameworks as well as addressing gender issues at the PPP project planning, design, implementation, and monitoring stages can lead to greater access for women to benefit from infrastructure and services.

PPPs can play an important role in addressing gender inequalities by advancing the development of infrastructure that mainstreams gender, promotes equality, empowers women, and fosters inclusive growth. To unlock the potential for gender-responsive PPPs, certain steps are needed. Firstly, awareness should be raised that women, because of existing gender and social norms, can face barriers in accessing infrastructure or the services it offers, and they may face heightened risks such as an increase in exposure to gender-based violence or sexual harassment due to the development of new infrastructure. This can directly contribute to the impact (negative or positive) that the project can have. Secondly, a PPP regulatory framework should be examined to see if it recognizes women as key stakeholders and users of infrastructure. Women's views are important to inform issues of access, location, and affordability that are relevant to PPP projects. These insights will help infrastructure design improve its usability and accessibility to all users, and will lead to the expansion of a larger user base for better outcomes. Upgrading the design of infrastructure and the services it offers can benefit women, not only as users but also through skills training or employment opportunities that projects can create.

While the influence of PPPs in closing key gender gaps is becoming increasingly evident, practical tools and know-how tailored to address gender issues in PPP projects are still lacking. This tool kit therefore aims to offer practical tips on what gender issues should be considered across the PPP development cycle and what gender actions can be taken for different infrastructure sectors in response. The tool kit is the first of its kind for ADB and aims to bring teams working on PPPs and gender equality closer in collaboration toward common objectives.

Samantha Hung
Director
Gender Equality Division
Climate Change and Sustainable
Development Department
Asian Development Bank

Adrian Torres
Director
Special Initiatives and Funds
Office of Markets Development and
Public–Private Partnership
Asian Development Bank

ACKNOWLEDGMENTS

This publication was prepared under the Asian Development Bank (ADB) regional technical assistance for Strengthening Project Preparation Capacity in Asia and the Pacific: Support for the Establishment of Enabling Environment for Public–Private Partnerships, funded by the Asia Pacific Project Preparation Facility (AP3F).

The tool kit was developed by the consultant, Ketevan Chkheidze, and the process was supervised and managed by Ichiro Aoki and Radhika Behuria from ADB's Office of Markets Development and Public–Private Partnership, in collaboration with Prabhjot Khan and Malika Shagazatova from ADB's Gender Equality Division under its Climate Change and Sustainable Development Department.

The report has benefited from the valuable inputs of the following peer reviewers from the ADB headquarters in Manila: Anne Valko Celestino, Ingrid Fitzgerald, Dhawal Jhamb, Rosemary Castillo Ong, and Amanda A. Satterly.

Other ADB colleagues also shared their perspectives, experience, and insights on how public–private partnership projects can better integrate gender equality issues, which contributed to the quality and usability of the tool kit. The publication team would like to convey its appreciation to these colleagues: Amer A. Chowdhury, Sheharyar Chughtai, Mohammed Azim Hashimi, Veronica Mendizabal Joffre, Claire Angeline Luczon, Mairi Macrae, Mary Alice G. Rosero, Euna Shim, Amanda Tan, and Francesco Tornieri. Sajid Chowdhury provided editorial and design support for the tool kit.

ABBREVIATIONS

ADB	Asian Development Bank
AP3F	Asia Pacific Project Preparation Facility
COVID-19	coronavirus disease
DMC	developing member country
ESIA	environmental and social impact assessment
MDB	multilateral development bank
O&M	operation and maintenance
OECD	Organisation for Economic Co-operation and Development
PPP	public–private partnership
SDG	Sustainable Development Goal

1
INTRODUCTION

Public–private partnership (PPP) refers to a contractual arrangement between public (national, state, provincial, or local) and private entities through which the skills, assets, and/or financial resources of each of the public and private sectors are allocated in a complementary manner, thereby sharing the risks and rewards, to provide optimal service delivery and value for money.[1]

While traditional infrastructure development has been implemented by governments alone, private sector engagement through PPP arrangements can bring in operational efficiency, budget optimization, technological innovation, international best practice, and overall value for money. PPPs can play an important role in advancing the development of infrastructure that facilitates economic activity, thereby reducing poverty in the short and long term.

PPPs have the potential to promote gender equality. Women are important stakeholders for PPP projects across these projects' development cycle, not only as users but also as planners, investors, constructors, and operators. Infrastructure projects with gender-inclusive design features can help to achieve better development results and make positive economic impact through an increase in use among women. Addressing gender issues in PPPs requires understanding of the basic links between gender equality issues and infrastructure development. Consideration of the intersection, gaps, and opportunities between gender and PPPs can help governments, the private sector, and development partners better plan, prepare, and implement PPP projects.

Why Gender Equality Matters for Public–Private Partnerships

Historically, the infrastructure needs of Asia and the Pacific have been massive. Earlier projections indicated that Asia will need to invest about $1.7 trillion per year in infrastructure until 2030 to maintain growth, challenge poverty, and respond to climate change.[2] Today, the needs are even larger, as many countries have set forth on their economic recovery after the coronavirus disease (COVID-19) pandemic. In the context of infrastructure development, however, not just quantity but also the quality of infrastructure matters. As many countries envisage building back better, infrastructure development must be carried out in a sustainable, resilient, and inclusive manner.

To this end, engagement of the private sector in infrastructure and service development is imperative. Private partners can bring in their knowledge, experience, efficiency, and capital to increase the number, as well as improve the quality, of infrastructure and services simultaneously. PPP is one of the most effective modalities to involve the private sector to work in partnership with the public sector.

---

1   Asian Development Bank (ADB). 2012. *Public–Private Partnership Operational Plan, 2012–2020: Realizing the Vision for Strategy 2020— The Transformational Role of Public–Private partnerships in Asian Development Bank Operations.* Manila. https://www.adb.org/sites/default/files/institutional-document/33671/ppp-operational-plan-2012-2020.pdf.

2   ADB. 2017. *Meeting Asia's Infrastructure Needs.* Manila. https://www.adb.org/sites/default/files/publication/227496/special-report-infrastructure.pdf.

Gender equality is an integral part of inclusive growth and should become central to the PPP agenda (Figure 1), particularly in the context of post-pandemic economic recovery. If infrastructure projects take gender considerations into account in their design and structure, they can meet the differing needs and priorities of men and women that stem from different roles and responsibilities in their households, communities, and societies. It would also maximize benefits of each project as more users would be captured, which leads to more stable public services provision. As a result, more projects can maximize value for money and build investors' confidence, which could further accelerate the pace of infrastructure development.

PPP = public–private partnership.
Source: Asian Development Bank.

Relevance of Gender Equality in the Development of Public–Private Partnership Infrastructure Projects

KEY MESSAGE

- **Infrastructure projects to be developed under PPP models can address key gender objectives and goals in each of the five areas of strategic focus within ADB's Strategy 2030:**
  (i)   Women's economic empowerment,
  (ii)   Gender equality in human development,
  (iii) Gender equality in decision-making and leadership,
  (iv)   Reduced time poverty of women, and
  (v)   Women's resilience to external shocks.

"Accelerating progress in gender equality" is one of the seven operational priorities of Strategy 2030 of the Asian Development Bank (ADB). To scale up support for gender equality, Strategy 2030 portrays five areas of strategic focus—(i) women's economic empowerment, (ii) gender equality in human development, (iii) gender equality in decision-making and leadership, (iv) reduced time poverty of women, and (v) women's resilience to external shocks—as highlighted in Figure 2.

Source: Asian Development Bank.

Women's economic empowerment. Infrastructure projects and the services they provide can empower women through provision of better access to public services, improvement in mobility, and offering of new employment opportunities if designed with gender-inclusive features.

Gender equality in human development. PPP modalities have become increasingly more common for social sector projects. Some examples of gender contribution in these areas include the following: (i) education projects can be designed to improve gender equality in completion rates, learning outcomes, and school-to-work transitions; (ii) health and social projects can address health needs of women and girls; and (iii) elder care services can be designed to ease women's family and care duties and meet the diverse needs of older women.

Gender equality in decision-making and leadership. Legal, institutional, and governance reforms can explore measures to remove gender-neutral or discriminatory provisions, enhance women's participation in public resource allocation and decision-making, and support leadership at all levels.

Reduced time poverty of women. Infrastructure services (e.g., transportation, remote access to public services) can help reduce women's burden and time involved in the management of livelihoods and unpaid domestic and care work. For women to have increased and better access to the infrastructure services, it is important to ensure users' safety. Well-designed infrastructure that considers gender-safe features (e.g., optimal lighting, setting up of escalators or elevators, protection of user identity) can address these issues.

Women's resilience to external shocks. ADB is separately supporting developing member countries (DMCs) in climate change and disaster risk management operations through infrastructure development. These operations will harness women's access to green jobs, climate-smart technologies, and participation in climate-related decision-making.

How to Use the Tool Kit

> **KEY MESSAGES**
>
> - **This tool kit was developed to serve as an entry point for anyone who is engaged in PPP operations and to integrate gender considerations in PPP projects throughout the development cycle.**
> - **The tool kit offers guidance at two levels:**
>   - (i) Helps tool kit users to become aware of how PPPs can offer more inclusive and gender-responsive infrastructure and services for broader benefit; and
>   - (ii) Presents practical approaches and application of gender considerations across the PPP development cycle, from early stages of project identification to project preparation and monitoring.

ADB has a number of tools to support gender mainstreaming across sectors. However, these tools are not tailored to PPPs. In response, this tool kit was developed as an entry point for anyone who is engaged in PPP operations to integrate gender considerations in PPP projects throughout the development cycle. The gender considerations in the tool kit are of advisory character and are meant to serve as recommendations. The tool kit offers a menu of options to promote gender equality and enhance PPP project outcomes.

The tool kit offers guidance at two levels: first, it helps tool kit users to become aware how PPPs can offer more inclusive and gender-responsive infrastructure and services for broader benefit; and second, it presents practical approaches and application of gender considerations across the PPP development cycle, from early stages of project identification to project preparation and monitoring. The tool kit highlights specific gender considerations for PPPs and good practice examples. It also offers a list of useful resources and sector considerations for more exploration by users.

2

CONCEPTUAL FRAMEWORK FOR GENDER INTEGRATION IN PUBLIC–PRIVATE PARTNERSHIPS

Key Bottlenecks for Gender Equality in Public–Private Partnership Infrastructure Projects

> ## KEY MESSAGE
>
> - **Key issues are slowing integration of gender considerations into PPPs:**
>   - (i) **Key issue 1.** Lack of awareness of the loss of opportunities for not integrating gender consideration, and the benefits of including women's perspectives in PPPs.
>   - (ii) **Key issue 2.** Women and men have different needs, experiences, and challenges that can define the outcome of projects.
>   - (iii) **Key issue 3.** Women are key users of infrastructure and its services, and their participation at all levels has positive outcomes; yet, their voices are often not heard at the community, executive, and decision-making levels.
>   - (iv) **Key issue 4.** Country commitments to address gender inequality can be supported through gender-inclusive policies, including legal and regulatory frameworks governing PPPs.
>   - (v) **Key issue 5.** Women's economic participation is limited, but their inclusion creates positive impacts for businesses and economies.

Infrastructure projects are often considered gender-neutral and not seen to specifically address gender gaps, inequalities, or differences.[3] Contrary to common perception, there are a number of ways that gender equality can be addressed through the development of infrastructure, particularly when PPP modalities are utilized.

Integration of gender considerations into PPPs has not progressed much because of five key issues and bottlenecks.

(i) **Key issue 1:** Lack of awareness of the loss of opportunities for not integrating gender consideration, and the benefits of including women's perspectives in public–private partnerships

While many stakeholders in PPP markets are aware that gender equality is a key development agenda, few are familiar with specific risks of losing opportunities by not integrating gender considerations in PPPs. In addition, most private investors have a misperception that integration of gender-inclusive design and features is only an additional cost factor and simply impairs their investment return. However, gender-inclusive PPPs can deliver certain benefits beyond social gains, such as revenue increases by capturing women as additional users. Raising stakeholders' awareness of both costs and income factors can enable them to appropriately conduct cost–benefit analyses of integration of gender-inclusive features, and it is the first step of gender actions in the field of PPP.

---

3   The term "gender-neutral" means that something is not associated with either women or men. It may refer to various aspects such as concepts or style of language. However, what is often perceived to be gender-neutral, including in areas of statistics or dissemination of data collected in reference to a population, often reflects gender blindness in practice (a failure to recognize gender specificities). European Institute for Gender Equality. Glossary and Thesaurus. https://eige.europa.eu/publications-resources/thesaurus/overview. More useful terms are provided in Appendix 1.

(ii) **Key issue 2:** Women and men have different needs, experiences, and challenges that can define the outcome of projects

Because of unequal distribution of and access to resources, opportunities, and power, women and men have different needs, experiences, and challenges.[4] These can be considered at the PPP projects' planning and design stages to enhance project outcomes. For instance, women and men have different transportation needs and utilization of transport services, which are influenced by social and economic status, travel patterns, use of transport mode, access to resources for travel, mobility patterns, and personal safety. Studies show that insufficient consideration of gender differences when planning and designing infrastructure can potentially exclude women from users' groups or perpetuate existing inequalities and create unintended and undesired outcomes.[5] This issue is not specific to the transport sector and can be observed in other sectors as well.

(iii) **Key Issue 3:** Women are key users of infrastructure and its services, and their participation at all levels has positive outcomes; yet, their voices are often not heard at the community, executive, and decision-making levels

Despite signs of improvement, women are underrepresented in all decision-making, and certain sectors have more glaring gender disparities. According to the Organisation for Economic Co-operation and Development (OECD), women make up only 16% of corporate boards of multinational enterprises, and the technology sector has the lowest representation at 12%.[6] Women's representation in politics in Asia and the Pacific is 20%, which is lower than the global average of 25%.[7] Historically, infrastructure development has been a male-dominated area, leaving women little or no space in investment decisions that affect their daily lives and well-being.[8] At the community level, a number of development organizations have started to target women in community interventions and consultations, recognizing that women's participation is vital to address women's needs and maximize impact of projects and programs.[9] While gender differences in leadership persist, PPP interventions can involve women in decision-making processes through stakeholder consultations.

4   European Institute for Gender Equality. Gender Mainstreaming Tools: Gender Analysis. https://eige.europa.eu/gender-mainstreaming/methods-tools/gender-analysis.

5   International Finance Corporation (IFC). 2012. *Gender Impact of Public–Private Partnerships: Literature Review Synthesis Report.* Consultant's report. https://ppp.worldbank.org/public-private-partnership/sites/ppp.worldbank.org/files/documents/PIDG-IFC_Gender%20Impact%20of%20Private%20Public%20Partnerships%20in%20Infrastructure.pdf.

6   OECD. 2020. Gender Equality: What Big Data Can Tell Us About Women on Boards. https://www.oecd.org/gender/data/what-big-data-can-tell-us-about-women-on-boards.htm.

7   United Nations Entity for Gender Equality and the Empowerment of Women (UN Women) Asia and the Pacific. Snapshot of Women's Leadership in Asia and the Pacific. https://asiapacific.unwomen.org/en/news-and-events/in-focus/csw/snapshot-of-womens-leadership-in-asia-and-the-pacific.

8   OECD. 2021. Women in Infrastructure: Selected Stocktaking of Good Practices for Inclusion of Women in Infrastructure. *OECD Public Governance Policy Papers.* No. 07. Paris: OECD Publishing. https://doi.org/10.1787/9eab66a8-en.

9   ADB. 2019. *Strategy 2030 Operational Plan for Priority 2: Accelerating Progress in Gender Equality, 2019–2024.* Manila. https://www.adb.org/sites/default/files/institutional-document/495956/strategy-2030-op2-gender-equality.pdf.

(iv)   **Key issue 4:** Country commitments to address gender inequality can be supported through gender-inclusive policies, including legal and regulatory frameworks governing public–private partnerships

Governments of almost all countries across Asia and the Pacific have made efforts to narrow gender gaps by adopting commitments and developing national policies and plans. However, because of lack of awareness, capacity, and resources, laws and policies are not properly implemented and operationalized. Meanwhile, laws and policies promoting gender equality are often stand-alone and are not aligned with the regulatory framework that governs PPPs.

As PPPs are strongly linked with a government's strategy and economic agenda, the role of government policies is crucial in addressing gender inclusion and women's empowerment. When setting up a new PPP framework or reform for an existing framework, gender gaps can be identified, and enabling conditions for gender-inclusive infrastructure development can be put in place.

(v)   **Key Issue 5:** Women's economic participation is limited, but their inclusion creates positive impacts for businesses and economies

PPPs have potential to improve women's economic participation through different approaches, such as by adopting gender-inclusive policies and practices in commercial investments, and promoting women in job and skills development opportunities, including in the infrastructure sector. Women's participation in economic activities can therefore contribute more to economic development if their potential is fully utilized.

Potential Risks and Opportunities of Gender Issues in Public–Private Partnership Projects

KEY MESSAGE

- **Failure to consider gender issues may increase the risk of exacerbating gender inequality. Consideration of gender issues creates opportunities to enhance project outcomes and to promote gender equality.**

PPP projects have potential to benefit women. However, not all PPP projects have gender-inclusive features. Projects without gender considerations may affect men and women differently, and not positively in some cases.

Failure to consider gender issues may increase the risk of exacerbating gender inequality. Consideration of gender issues creates opportunities to enhance project outcomes and to promote gender equality.

These risks and opportunities include

(i)   **A risk of exacerbating gender inequality.** While PPPs are largely promoted as one possible procurement modality for infrastructure projects and services, they do not often recognize gender differences, despite being built for quality public services.[10] As a result, projects may unintentionally exclude or further constrain women's access to infrastructure and its services, and may also exacerbate gender inequalities. For instance, risks of gender-based and sexual violence can increase with labor influx and civil works brought in through PPP arrangements of infrastructure (footnote 5). A PPP infrastructure project can exacerbate women's economic lower status by not engaging them in employment opportunities or by employing them in traditionally feminized roles. In addition, if infrastructure does not consider usability by women, it may constrain women's access and significantly undermine the anticipated and desired socioeconomic benefits. While most countries have protection laws in place, such laws and systems may not always be effective to prevent such risks in PPP projects. Therefore, project planners and practitioners should address these risks early in the development cycle to avoid unintended consequences for women.

(ii)   **An opportunity to enhance project outcomes.** If PPP projects analyze and identify gender differences as well as potential benefits and positive impacts that the projects can make in terms of participation, access, safety, and/or affordability for women and men, such analysis can address the inequalities through informed gender-responsive project design. If projects are responsive to gender differences, they can improve access and usability of the infrastructure and its services, thereby improving overall project outcomes. Another key area where PPP projects can make a big difference is through creating opportunities for employment and/or income-generating activities for women. This can be enabled through improving employment conditions, establishing nondiscriminatory and equal opportunities measures and policies, and supporting women to participate as part of the supply chains.

(iii)   **An opportunity to promote gender equality.** Most countries in Asia and the Pacific have national or subnational legislation and/or policies as part of international commitments to ensure equality between women and men and to promote women's economic, social, and political empowerment. However, implementation of commitments has been slow because of lack of awareness and also low levels of resources and capacity. Because of social and cultural factors and norms, women continue to face inequalities and discrimination in practice, leading to their absence in areas such as decision-making and leadership, limited access to services, heavy household responsibilities, and low levels of employment and career advancement.[11] PPP projects have potential to offer solutions to these issues. Gender-responsive features can be integrated in the design and concept of each infrastructure project to be developed under PPP modalities. Upon completion, women can benefit from these projects through the provision of gender-inclusive services and/or additional employment opportunities. These can contribute to DMCs' gender equality commitments and increase the role of PPPs as catalysts for positive economic and social outcomes.

---

10   M. J. Romero and J. Gideon. 2019. *Can Public–Private Partnerships Deliver Gender Equality?* Briefing Paper. Brussels: European Network on Debt and Development / London: Gender and Development Network / Nairobi: African Women's Development and Communication Network. https://assets.nationbuilder.com/eurodad/pages/443/attachments/original/1590686869/Can_public-private_partnerships_deliver_gender_equality_.pdf?1590686869.

11   ADB. 2016. *Vision for Gender Equality in Asia and Pacific by 2030: Possible Future Directions for Asian Development Bank's Gender Work.* Background Paper. Manila. https://www.adb.org/sites/default/files/institutional-document/323951/adb-bgpaper-gender-2030.pdf.

Box 1 presents a good practice for promoting a safe and gender-inclusive public transportation system in the Philippines.

Box 1

Good Practice Approach: Addressing Gender Risks—Operation and Maintenance of the High-Priority Bus System in Davao City, Philippines

The Davao High-Priority Bus System project, supported by the Asia Pacific Project Preparation Facility (AP3F), aims to provide an accessible, inclusive, and safe public transportation system that includes procurement of buses, bus stops, terminals, depots, and pedestrian crossing facilities for commuters and workers. Gender analysis was carried out at the project's conceptualization stage, which confirmed that the Philippines has a comprehensive gender quality legislation and policies in place. These include the country's Harmonized Gender and Development Guidelines, which provide direction on how to integrate gender considerations in project design, implementation, and monitoring and evaluation across all sectors. Despite these policies, gender inequality and gaps remain. During the initial study, some risks and benefits were identified related to users' travel patterns and economic opportunities.

To not actualize potential gender risks, a series of gender actions will be recommended by the Asian Development Bank's Office of Public–Private Partnership. These gender actions are considered at two different levels:

(i)   At the project level, the operation and maintenance (O&M) contractor will be advised to maintain continuity and provision of safety and accessibility features in buses, terminals, depots, and bus stops by developing relevant tools to measure user satisfaction with safety and security. The O&M contractor will be also advised to promote policies and trainings for workers, security personnel, and frontline employees related to ensuring safety of women and girls; and to ensure that adequate signage and information about prevention and addressing of sexual harassment is provided (in line with Davao City's information and education campaign).

Upgraded transport technology. ADB support to Davao City in the Philippines will enable modernization of the city's transport sector (photo by ADB).

(ii) At the organizational level, the O&M contractor will be advised to to promote gender-inclusive workplace policies and practices, such as policies and practices for prevention of sexual exploitation, abuse, and harassment.

The contractor will also be recommended to place relevant employment targets for women in its total O&M workforce, and to maintain disaggregated data (e.g., sex, age, disability) about applicants and hired employees.

These approaches can help avoid safety risks for women and girls, enhance their mobility and accessibility to transport, promote employment and a women-friendly workplace, and reduce workplace risks.

Source: Asian Development Bank. List of Gender Actions Document for Capacity Building, Project Preparation, and Project Performance Support: Operation and Maintenance for the Davao City High-Priority Bus System, Republic of the Philippines. Unpublished.

Guiding Principles and Main Approaches for Integrating Gender in Public–Private Partnership Project Development

> ### ○ KEY MESSAGE ○
>
> - **Integration of gender equality considerations into PPP revolves around two principles of gender mainstreaming:**
>   (i)   Conduct gender-specific review and analysis at the PPP project development cycle; and
>   (ii) Incorporate gender-inclusive features into the design of the PPP framework, institutional structure, architecture of projects, and/or the services that projects deliver.

The core guiding principles of PPP operations for ADB are streamlined across three key stages—upstream, midstream, and downstream—including capacity building of the government, promotion of an enabling environment, and transaction advisory services and financing. At each stage of the PPP development cycle, specific gender-inclusive features can be recommended. However, the incorporation of gender considerations has not been very common largely because of limited understanding about the significance of integrating gender considerations, lack of prioritization of gender aspects, or the perception that they can create additional costs for a project. By integrating gender considerations at early stages, certain project risks, which may be difficult to eliminate at a later stage, can be mitigated. Understanding why gender equality matters for the PPP development cycle and applying gender considerations to each stage can play a crucial role in maximizing benefits of project outcomes for all.

Integration of gender equality considerations into PPP revolves around two principles of gender mainstreaming:

(i)   Conduct gender-specific review and analysis within the PPP project development cycle. The purpose of the gender analysis is to identify needs and reveal potential gender entry points that may cut across PPP legal and regulatory frameworks, gender-inclusive policies, capacity building, stakeholder and community consultations, and gender entry points for projects for private sector implementation.

(ii) Incorporate gender-inclusive features into the design of the PPP framework, institutional structure, architecture of projects, and/or the services that projects deliver. Implement them through gender actions, and monitor impacts.

Both of the principles are essential. These principles are aligned with the overall gender mainstreaming principles, as well as with ADB's Policy on Gender and Development (Box 2).[12] Gender mainstreaming is an important consideration for ADB's lending operations (e.g., loans to government or private sector), but it is not considered a mandatory measure for PPPs. However, the above principles can also adhere to the PPP project development cycle and allow for gender equality considerations at various stages.

Box 2
Gender Mainstreaming in ADB Operations

Job opportunities for women. Rosalina, 29, works in the "Turkmenbashi Tekstil Kompleksi," the biggest textile factory in Central Asia. Over 3,000 people, 95% women, work in the textile factory (photo by ADB).

The Asian Development Bank (ADB) adopts gender mainstreaming as a key strategy for promoting gender equality. This requires gender concerns to be treated as a crosscutting theme influencing all social and economic processes. For ADB, "mainstreaming" requires explicit integration of gender considerations into all aspects of ADB operations. This also entails ensuring the consideration of gender issues at all stages of the project cycle. ADB's Policy on Gender and Development recommends that gender disparities be directly addressed through design of programs and projects with specific gender features and targets that deliver gender equality and women's empowerment benefits, such as improved access to social services, economic and financial resources and opportunities, basic rural and urban infrastructure, and/or enhanced voices and rights.

Source: ADB. 2023. Gender Equality and Women's Empowerment in ADB Operations. *Operations Manual.* OM C2. Manila.

Opportunities for integration of gender into PPPs are intertwined across the PPP development cycle, in which government and private sector partners both have crucial roles. At the macro level, integration of gender-inclusive features into PPP laws, policies, and regulations will bring about commitments that can be carried out by key stakeholders, both from the public and the private sectors. In addition, these legal requirements give guidance to market participants of how gender equality can be addressed through specific actions. Based on these legal requirements, infrastructure and its services can be designed to address gender inclusion and provide practical mechanisms to amplify positive outcomes of PPP projects for various groups of people. Some of these gender provisions can be applied and monitored through specific key performance indicators for the private sector entity, by ensuring that these are aligned with DMCs' national gender policy commitments and other legislative frameworks. The areas of gender considerations and/or indicators may vary depending on the sector, the project scope, and the role of a contractor.

Box 3 presents a good practice for integrating gender in the project design of Uzbekistan's national solar program.

Box 3

Good Practice Approach: Integrating Gender in the Project Design—Uzbekistan's 1-Gigawatt National Solar Program (Phase 3 Solar Project)

A gender review was conducted as part of a of technical assistance project supported by the Asia Pacific Project Preparation Facility (AP3F). The review revealed that, despite progress in gender equality policies and initiatives in Uzbekistan, challenges remained for women with regard to their active participation in the energy sector. Therefore, gender actions were included in the project preparation technical assistance. More specifically, key performance indicators were included in the concession agreement, requiring the private entity to

(i)   integrate gender-differentiated needs and priorities in the project design;

(ii) apply principles of nondiscrimination, prevention of gender-based violence, sexual exploitation, abuse and harassment, response mechanisms, and equal opportunity for independent power producers;

(iii) promote gender equality in the energy sector, including gender-responsive human resources policies and women-friendly infrastructure in the workplace; and

(iv) promote equal employment opportunities and gender equality, with the potential to set a defined target to promote women's employment.

Source: Asian Development Bank. 2022. List of Gender Actions Document for Project Preparation Assistance: 1-Gigawatt National Solar Program–Phase 3 Solar Project, Republic of Uzbekistan. Unpublished.

Roles Expected for Promoting Gender Integration in Public–Private Partnerships

○ **KEY MESSAGE** ○

- **Integration of gender considerations requires coordinated action. Various parties, roles, and skills can contribute to the integration of gender in the project and cycle, and each party has a specific role:**
  (i) **Public sector.** The role of governments is to set up and define a robust framework to analyze and identify country-specific gender issues, develop strategies to address the issues, and operationalize gender actions. Governments also monitor and supervise the progress of gender actions carried out by both the public and the private sectors, and they provide feedback on whether the efforts have been made on the right path.
  (ii) **Private sector.** Private partners put policies, strategies, and ideas into action. They bring in knowledge, experience, and/or skill sets of international best practice and adopt innovative and efficient approaches.
  (iii) **Multilateral development banks.** These banks can provide leadership, tools, guidelines, and advice to help both public and private parties include gender equality considerations in PPP projects. They can also help align stakeholders from the public and the private sectors, and set standards for gender-sensitive market interventions.

Integration of gender considerations into PPP requires coordinated action. Each party can play a specific role and contribute vital skills (Figure 3).

Public sector. The role of governments is to set up and define a robust framework to analyze and identify country-specific gender issues, develop strategies to address issues, and operationalize gender actions. Governments also monitor and supervise the progress of gender actions carried out by both the public and the private sectors, and they provide feedback on whether efforts have been made on the right path. The public sector is responsible for setting the normative framework by integrating gender considerations into policies, systems, and regulations. It should also be responsible for collection, storage, and sharing of sex-disaggregated data that key stakeholders can refer to and utilize. For this purpose, governments should be aware of gender inequality issues and concerns. In this regard, building governments' capacity on how to address gender equality issues is important for guidance, setting a strong regulatory reform, and gender mainstreaming.

Private sector. Private partners put policies, strategies, and ideas into action. They bring knowledge, experience, and/or skill sets of international best practice and adopt innovative and efficient approaches. They can maximize positive outcomes and contribute toward gender equality in PPP projects. They are expected to carry out gender actions and comply with governments' plans, strategies, policies, and international best practice. Adopting gender sensitivity and mainstreaming not only allows private sector companies to meet requirements, but also provides benefits to the project as well as to the company.

Multilateral development banks. Investing in women's and girls' health, education, and livelihood opportunities is critical for sustainable and resilient economies. Multilateral development banks (MDBs) have a role in delivering initiatives that contribute to gender equality and women's empowerment through PPPs. MDBs can provide the necessary leadership, tools, guidelines, and advice to help both public and private parties include gender equality considerations in PPP projects. MDBs can also help align stakeholders from the public and the private sectors and set standards for gender-sensitive market interventions.

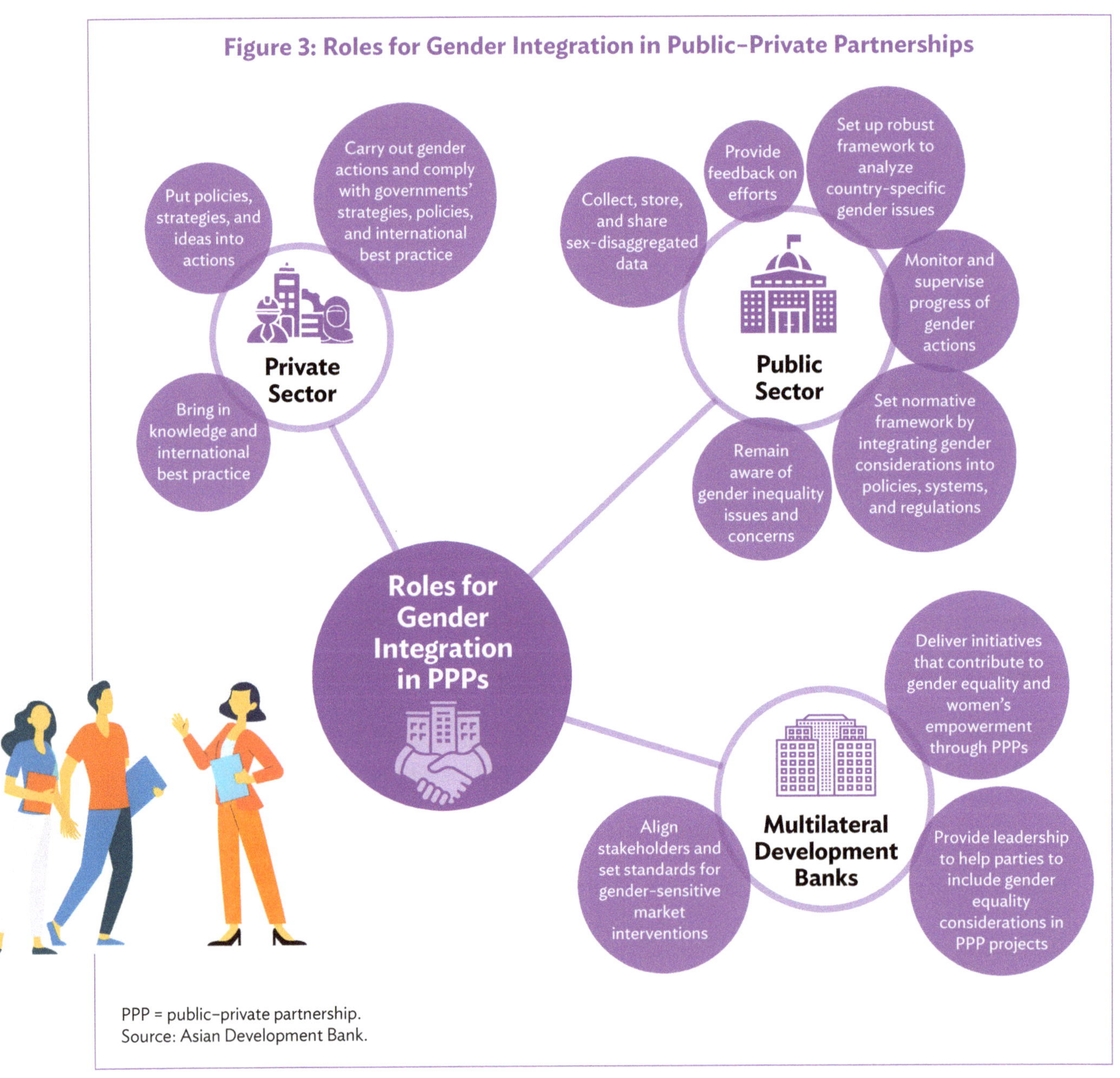

PPP = public–private partnership.
Source: Asian Development Bank.

3
INTEGRATION
OF GENDER IN
PUBLIC–PRIVATE
PARTNERSHIP
PROJECTS AND
THROUGHOUT
THEIR
DEVELOPMENT
CYCLE

Public–Private Partnership Operations and Potential Gender Considerations at a Glance

> **◦ KEY MESSAGE ◦**
>
> • **Gender considerations can be integrated across three main pillars of ADB's PPP operations:**
>   (i)   Upstream assistance: advocacy and the development of a PPP-enabling environment (e.g., capacity building, policy and institutional reforms);
>   (ii) Midstream assistance: project preparation (e.g., transaction advisory services); and
>   (iii) Downstream assistance: project financing.

The focus of upstream support is to assist governments to create a conducive enabling environment for PPPs. The private sector is involved in midstream and downstream support and therefore requires building a strong business case. Gender considerations can be integrated across the three main pillars of ADB's PPP operations (footnote 1), and this tool kit recommends practical approaches to their application.

Customized approaches are recommended for each pillar, corresponding to the type of assistance offered at each stage of the PPP development cycle (Figure 4).

Figure 4: Approaches for Gender Mainstreaming in Public–Private Partnership Operations

Upstream

Development of Enabling Environment

- Raise awareness
- Build capacity of government officials
- Develop or reform institutional and regulatory framework
- Establish central PPP unit and PPP database
- Develop pipeline, and conduct initial screening

Major Instruments

- Knowledge products
- Technical assistance
- Policy-based loans

Gender-Inclusive Approaches

Explore facilitating factors for integration of gender into PPPs

Policy scan through gender lens, which analyzes legal and regulatory framework for PPP and their linkages with existing gender policies and legal frameworks

Capacity-building and stakeholder mapping to reveal potential gender risks and opportunities that may arise during implementation

Midstream

Project Preparation

- Conceptualize and define PPP projects
- Provide project preparation assistance for PPP projects to award concession to private partners

Major Instruments

- Transaction advisory service
- Technical assistance

Gender-Inclusive Approaches

Identify gender issues and entry points and potential impact of project on women and men

Identify specific requirements for PPP projects (for bidding, procurement, SEAH prevention)

Support gender analysis to inform client government of potential risks and opportunities related to integration of gender aspects

Propose relevant gender actions and measures for project

Identify right private partner for award of concession that can manage gender risks and create opportunities for women

Downstream

Project Financing

- Structure effective project finance
- Provide long-term financing
- Catalyze commercial finance
- Provide credit enhancement products

Major Instruments

- Nonsovereign financing
- Sovereign financing
- Guarantees

Gender-Inclusive Approaches

Include gender equality issues in financing structure

Include gender-sensitive monitoring of agreed and renegotiated progress and results

PPP = public–private partnership; SEAH = sexual exploitation, abuse, and harassment.
Source: Asian Development Bank.

Gender Actions for Upstream Assistance

> **○ KEY MESSAGE ○**
>
> - **The following gender actions are suggested for upstream assistance:**
>   (i)   Raise awareness on why and how gender equality is relevant for PPPs,
>   (ii)   Build governments' capacity to promote gender equality,
>   (iii) Highlight and advocate for benefits of considering gender for infrastructure projects,
>   (iv)   Scope out existing gender policies and gender-sensitive frameworks, and
>   (v)   Integrate gender-related regulations into PPP frameworks.

The first step in upstream assistance includes advocacy, enhancement of knowledge management, and development of government capacity for PPPs. These interventions can also raise awareness of gender equality and how to mainstream gender issues in PPPs across different sectors. In most countries, there is limited institutional capacity related to gender, including knowledge of gender equality, relevance of gender equality to PPP, and how issues should be addressed in legal frameworks.

PPP legal frameworks refer to all laws and legislations that regulate PPP along its development cycle. Therefore, any gender provisions integrated in these policies can facilitate more inclusive approaches and subsequent outcomes. While most countries have gender equality policies and frameworks, they are rarely linked to or aligned with PPP frameworks. There are also limited dedicated resources and staff to support gender mainstreaming in organizations, as well as a lack of gender-inclusive decision-making processes.

To address these issues, the following gender actions are suggested:

(i)   Raise awareness of why and how gender equality is relevant for public–private partnerships

When PPP awareness-raising support is offered, gender equality considerations for the project can be highlighted. This is the first opportunity to raise awareness and sensitize the government partner on topics such as why gender equality is important, why sex-disaggregated data should be collected, how a gender assessment can improve PPP infrastructure outcomes, and how to identify and address gender issues at different stages of the PPP development cycle. This is also an opportunity to promote gender parity and diversity within the unit responsible for undertaking PPPs, e.g., by improving and introducing gender-inclusive workplace policies and practices.

(ii)   Build government's capacity to promote gender equality

After the government has developed basic awareness of gender equality and major issues, capacity development support can be offered to government officials to help them understand what actions can improve gender equality in the country. Specialized gender expertise can be brought into the institution or department responsible for PPPs to build staff capacity. Importantly, data collection training can be included in the project, as unavailability of sex-disaggregated data is often recognized as a bottleneck to devising gender-responsive interventions.

This is also an opportunity to promote the engagement of female staff members in overall capacity-building initiatives for PPP or other related units. It is also important to ensure no all-male staff trainings and that a minimum number of women staff are engaged in capacity-building support so that gender gaps are not perpetuated inadvertently. Meanwhile, gender champions within PPP institutions can be nominated to push a gender equality agenda in PPP-related activities. Box 4 presents a good practice for governance and capacity-building support in Lao People's Democratic Republic.

Box 4

Good Practice Approach: Capacity-Building Support—Governance and Capacity Development of the Public Sector Management Program in the Lao People's Democratic Republic (Subprograms 1 and 2)

The Governance and Capacity Development in Public Sector Management Program Grant Project supported by the Asian Development Bank (ADB) had a strong focus on establishing and strengthening an enabling environment (e.g., policy, legal, and regulatory) for public–private partnerships (PPPs) in the Lao People's Democratic Republic. Among other issues, the project facilitated development of a business case for gender equality in selected PPP projects and developed gender actions through sample gender action plans (for health and education projects). Gender guidelines and checklists were also prepared. Gender-responsive targets and actions were mainstreamed into the PPP process, particularly in due diligence to support preparation of several cases for proposed PPP projects.

An important aspect of the capacity-building support was the training of the National Commission for the Advancement of Women staff. A pool of trainers was created to support topics of gender, addressing gender in human resource management and developing a gender mainstreaming manual. Among other capacity-building initiatives under the project, central and provincial government staff were trained on state land leases and concession models, investment contract management, environmental and social impact assessments, financial analysis for investment proposals, and investment contract negotiation. This training also included appraisal techniques (financial and economic analysis, including social, gender, and risk assessments) to screen, award, monitor, and exercise effective oversight of contracts and concession agreements for state lands.

Source: ADB. 2021. *Completion Report: Governance and Capacity Development in Public Sector Management Program (Subprograms 1 and 2) in Lao People's Democratic Republic*. Manila.

(iii)   Highlight and advocate for benefits of considering gender for infrastructure projects

Women are an important stakeholder in all infrastructure processes, and their roles as users of infrastructure and its services should be highlighted, as their insights can inform projects and can generate positive outcomes for the project. Use of sector tip sheets can identify clear benefits over the cost of a gendered approach as well as the advantages of considering gender differences in project planning and design.[13] Although it occurs at an early stage of PPP project development, and a full cost–benefit analysis may not be feasible, benefits of including women from a user perspective can be better understood by project planners to meet women's infrastructure needs.

---

[13]   ADB. Gender Tip Sheets. https://www.adb.org/documents/series/gender-tip-sheets?page=1.

(iv) Scope out existing gender policies and gender-sensitive frameworks

To advise on integrating gender policies into PPPs, it is critical to analyze the structure and framework of the existing legislations and identify the areas of potential alignment. The following guiding questions are helpful to explore these intersections:

(a) Has the country adopted international commitments for gender equality?
(b) Are country-specific laws, regulations, and policies gender-inclusive?
(c) Are sector policies gender-inclusive?
(d) Is there an existing PPP legal framework? Does it have any reference to gender policies or regulations? Alternatively, is there specific country guidance or policy that could help guide PPPs?
(e) Given the prevalent gender issues and challenges in the DMC, are additional policies needed to protect women's interests?

Most countries develop specific laws and regulations on gender that are aligned with international commitments and frameworks. A total of 189 countries around the world have ratified the Convention on the Elimination of All Forms of Discrimination Against Women, which is a guiding international framework and legislative tool upon which countries base their gender equality policies and institutions.[14] Another important international commitment for states are the Sustainable Development Goals (SDGs), which form a global blueprint for countries to achieve holistic development. SDG 5 is dedicated to pursuing gender equality as an essential foundation for a prosperous and sustainable world. The commitments to the SDGs have urged countries to undertake actions and measure their progress for gender equality, and this urgency has created many positive developments across the public and private sectors.[15] For each country to fully meet their international commitment, a link between gender equality and PPP in regulatory frameworks is needed. A policy scan is the first step of the series of gender-related regulatory reform.

(v) Integrate gender-related regulations into public–private partnership frameworks

Laws and regulations on gender equality are mostly isolated from PPP frameworks. As PPP frameworks define and govern PPP planning and implementation processes throughout the whole development cycle, identifying intersections between stand-alone gender equality laws and PPP regulations can be useful. More robust and inclusive country laws and policies can allow more opportunities for promoting gender considerations in PPP frameworks. As more countries are advocating inclusive growth, gender equality measures could be embodied as an integral part of the overall PPP frameworks (Box 5 provides an example in the Philippines), for instance in the following areas:

(a) **Project screening and prioritization.** Project screening criteria normally focus on economic and financial benefits of pipeline projects. Most project screening guidelines and/or regulations include criteria to assess whether the potential project may lead to positive impact for gender equality or lead to potential risks that may exacerbate existing inequalities. Gender can be included as a specific criterion in the screening process to emphasize potential gender benefits (both direct and indirect benefits) at an early stage, particularly if also contingent with the sector or infrastructure strategies of a country.

---

14   United Nations. 1979. *Convention on the Elimination of All Forms of Discrimination Against Women*. New York. https://www.un.org/womenwatch/daw/cedaw/.

15   UN Women. 2018. *Turning Promises into Actions: Gender Equality in the 2030 Agenda for Sustainable Development*. New York. https://www.unwomen.org/en/digital-library/publications/2018/2/gender-equality-in-the-2030-agenda-for-sustainable-development-2018.

Box 5

Good Practice Approach: Integrating Gender into the Public–Private Partnership Legal Framework—The Case of the Philippines

The National Government Agencies Public–Private Partnership (PPP) Guidebook of the Philippines provides detailed guidance to national government agencies in undertaking and managing PPP projects. The guidebook provides case studies, best practices, and lessons learned, and it includes the following gender considerations:

(i)   The discussion of technical risks includes social and gender impacts.

(ii) The guidebook acknowledges that gender equality should be promoted as part of potential project impact.

(iii) It calls for the integration of gender in feasibility studies as one consideration in addressing gender equality issues and addressing barriers of access, especially for marginalized sectors including women and people with disabilities.

(iv) PPP Governing Board Resolution No. 2018-12-02 of the Philippines provides guidance on integrating social and gender concerns in PPP projects at all levels. Gender provisions in the document are consistent with government laws and policies on gender, and are built on best practice considerations.

(v)   Finally, these guidelines also include a gender mainstreaming element in the phase when PPP projects are being evaluated for eligibility.

Source: Government of the Philippines, Public–Private Partnership Center. 2019. *NGA PPP Guidebook*. Quezon City. https://ppp.gov.ph/wp-content/uploads/2019/01/PPP_PUB_NGA-Guidebook_2018Dec.pdf.

(b) **Data collection.** Sex-disaggregated data is critical to understanding the differences in the lived experiences of women and men. However, the collection of such data at each project level may decelerate project development and become counterproductive. As a solution, PPP frameworks may incorporate provisions that require each line ministry to identify and collect sex-disaggregated data needed for their projects, or to use the most recent data to analyze and offer gender benefits. Such data should be archived in a central database and made available to implementing agencies or their advisors.

(c) **Due diligence.** Most countries require some due diligence to be conducted. Aligned with DMC laws and regulations, an environmental and social impact assessment (ESIA) could be required as part of overall due diligence. This is also an opportunity to understand women's needs as well as identify specific gender gaps. International development partners and finance institutions can mainstream this by including gender analysis in the ESIA for projects that they support, even if not explicitly required by regulation or by the client. The terms of reference of the ESIA specialist can include collection of sex-disaggregated data and exploration of questions to reveal potential gender issues and/or impacts in the questionnaire data to inform baseline studies (feasibility and/or prefeasibility) and ensure women's needs are captured, include women in stakeholder consultations at the community or project level, and analyze data to see gender differences with relation to the project to advise the potential gender actions. Where possible, gender specialists can be included in due diligence processes to provide gender analysis and recommend potential gender actions. A detailed terms of reference for a gender specialist is provided in Appendix 2.

(d) **Conceptualization.** Before pipeline projects are selected, approval by relevant authorities may be required in some countries (e.g., cabinet, Parliament, or ministry of finance). In these countries, it may be useful to make gender-inclusive aspects a requirement for approval. Based on approval, infrastructure architecture, or the services it provides, must be designed to include technical specifications that actualize gender benefits envisaged in its concept. Putting this approach into practice may be difficult in countries where gender policies are not robust. In such countries, it may be easier to start with the prioritization of projects with gender-inclusive elements.

Gender Actions for Midstream Assistance

○ KEY MESSAGES ○

- **Midstream assistance provides transaction advisory support to assist host country governments to prepare and conduct public tenders for contract award.**
- **Midstream assistance covers particularly critical stages to ensure that gender considerations are incorporated into project designs.**

The focus of midstream assistance is to assist governments in the procurement and delivery of public assets as well as public services through private sector engagement in a fair and transparent manner. The ultimate goal is to deliver commercially feasible projects to the market and have governments achieve commercial close (i.e., award of concession). Midstream assistance is considered a critical stage, particularly because gender equality issues are identified and integrated into the project design and structure at this stage. Certain considerations that are relevant to gender inclusiveness should be explored and adopted in these processes to the extent feasible.

Prior to the public tender, support is also offered to define key objectives, expected outcomes, and fit-for-purpose structure of the project as a concept. Project definition is an important step in the midstream approach, which is often provided back-to-back with transaction advisory. Gender considerations can be applied while providing comprehensive transaction advisory support (including project definition) by involving a gender specialist through gender review and analysis that could help capture the potential gender issues and benefits and enhance positive development impact of a PPP project.

An example of gender review and analysis is provided in Box 6, while Figure 5 presents the gender actions that can be taken for midstream assistance.

Box 6

Good Practice Approach: Gender Review of the Project Definition and Project Preparation Assistance—The Solar Public–Private Partnership Project in Maldives

A gender review was conducted as part of a of technical assistance project supported by the Asia Pacific Project Preparation Facility (AP3F), which highlighted the international commitments and government policies and laws in Maldives to translate its commitment for gender equality outcomes in social, economic, and political spheres. The National Gender Equality Policy, 2019 provides overall policy direction for gender mainstreaming. Maldives also has several targeted legal and regulatory provisions to protect and empower women in the private sector and promote women-friendly workplace practices.

The review highlighted that despite these efforts, sociocultural norms and gendered division of labor continue to influence access to resources and opportunities, particularly for women in Maldives. Gender issues in energy were also observed. While men and women have different energy uses and needs, women's perspectives are missed from planning and decision-making in the sector. A significant gender gap in employment rates persists, particularly in the energy sector, largely because of underrepresentation of women in science, technology, engineering, and mathematics programs.

 The government is focusing on increasing the pool of women that are ready for employment opportunities in the energy sector. To this end, support offered by the AP3F provided an opportunity to build on training and educational activities that promote gender equality and inclusiveness. The prospect of privatization, brought in through the AP3F technical assistance, especially in the context of new technologies, has the potential to increase new entrepreneurship opportunities for women in the long run. As part of the AP3F support, relevant gender provisions have been included in the concessionaire agreement of the private sector company to ensure inclusive and safe workplace practices and to promote employment opportunities for women. Also, in recognition of the large opportunity that the expansion of the solar sector provides in Maldives, a regional good practice paper was developed to highlight examples from other countries and identify entry points to promote women's employment in the country's solar sector. This paper has been presented to the client and included in the data room as part of the documentation shared with bidders.

Source: Asian Development Bank. 2022. List of Gender Actions Document for Project Definition and Preparation Assistance: Solar Public–Private Partnership Project, Republic of Maldives. Unpublished.

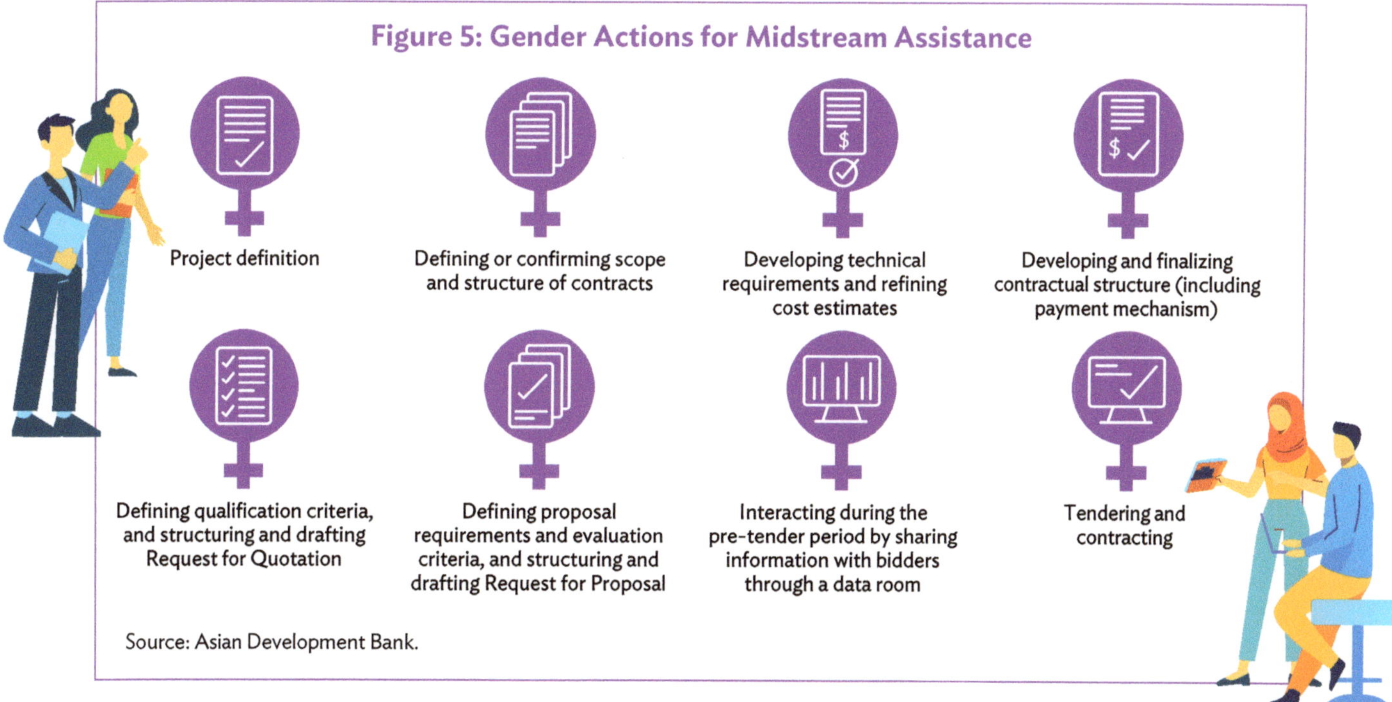

Figure 5: Gender Actions for Midstream Assistance

Source: Asian Development Bank.

Table 1 offers a summary of gender points of entry that a PPP project may consider for gender mainstreaming across the project cycle, using the transport sector as an example.[16]

Table 1: Gender Mainstreaming Points of Entry for Public–Private Partnership Projects
(Example of the Transport Sector)

Gender Design Features and Actions (What?)	Relevance to the Project	Approaches for PPP Projects (How?)	Alignment with Operational Priority 2 Strategic Priorities[a] or Gender Tag
TRANSPORT			
Project Planning Stage			
Ensure the PPP project considers women's and men's priorities for the transport sector	Inclusive and evidence-based planning	Identify and document needs and constraints of women related to the project, including for access and affordability of transport and services, capacity building, and other related issues Design infrastructure services that address women's needs, in particular accessibility to and affordability of transport services	2.3: Gender equality in decision-making and leadership enhanced
Project Implementation Stage			
Address women's accessibility to and affordability of transport services	Improved access to and affordability of infrastructure and services	Establish public transport schedules and pricing systems that respond to the needs of women and girl users, including affordable off-peak, multiple trip, and group traveler ticketing	2.4: Women's time poverty and drudgery reduced 2.1: Women's economic empowerment increased
Include physical infrastructure in PPP project design for women's safe mobility	Improved safety and mobility features for users	Invest in specific safety measures for women and girls, such as lighting across stations, improved signage on streets, and information for sexual harassment and/or gender-based violence hotlines Priority seating for pregnant women or women-only train compartments Use of GPS or other technology for mapping sexual harassment in public transport and creating awareness of transport staff on sexual harassment Promote context-specific actions, such as a sari guard attached to escalators (in South Asia) Ensure elevators are designed for ease of access for baby carriages	2.5: Women's resilience to external shocks strengthened
Employ women in different types of jobs (PPP project, private sector company)	Diversified workforce and empowerment of women	Establish number and share of women's employment by the project company (if feasible), develop internship programs for women to build a future talent pipeline, and establish mentorship programs for young women employees	2.1: Women's economic empowerment increased 2.3: Gender equality in decision-making and leadership enhanced

continued on next page

---

[16]   Gender points of entry across different sectors are provided in Appendix 3.

Table 1 *continued*

Gender Design Features and Actions (What?)	Relevance to the Project	Approaches for PPP Projects (How?)	Alignment with Operational Priority 2 Strategic Priorities[a] or Gender Tag
Target women in capacity building, including technical or other training under the project	Enhancing skills and diversifying the future workforce in the sector	Set number and share for women's inclusion (e.g., skills training; managerial; or other capacity-building initiatives, like gender awareness) Provide scholarships for students in the transport sector or set targets for women internship opportunities	2.2: Gender equality in human development enhanced
Promote women's livelihoods and entrepreneurship	Increased economic opportunities	Invest in public transport commercial hubs at stations, along roads, and at similar locations, allocating reserved shop spaces for women's businesses	2.1: Women's economic empowerment increased

GPS = global positioning system, PPP = public–private partnership.

[a] More details on the pillars and subpillars of the Asian Development Bank's Strategy 2030 Operational Plan for Priority 2 are provided here: Asian Development Bank. 2019. *Strategy 2030 Operational Plan for Priority 2: Accelerating Progress in Gender Equality, 2019–2024.* Manila. https://www.adb.org/sites/default/files/institutional-document/495956/strategy-2030-op2-gender-equality.pdf.

Source: Asian Development Bank.

(i)   Project definition

Before a PPP project is publicly tendered, it undergoes project definition processes. In these processes, details of the contract scope, technical requirements, and overall costs are examined and validated. These processes also include financial projection, a prefeasibility study, and market sounding. Based on these assessments, the project scope and structure are defined, and a set of PPP options is proposed.

During the project definition processes, an initial gender assessment can be conducted to identify areas where the planned project can contribute to gender equality. Specific information on gender gaps at this stage can inform whether a project has potential to promote gender equality and women's empowerment. Some of these considerations are assessed further at the subsequent project preparation stage.

To this end, a prefeasibility study can include requirements for identification of gender equality and women empowerment issues. These early-stage analyses do not require in-depth gender analysis. The objective is to understand general gender equality issues related to the sector or the project.

Data required for early-stage gender analyses may be identified in a data archive that the governments have developed if they have nominated a ministry or agency as the main party responsible for the collection of sex-disaggregated data. Alternatively, ADB's regional offices may have existing databases for their sovereign and nonsovereign projects, gender sector diagnostics, and country gender assessments. If no data exists, then a data collection exercise as part of feasibility studies can be considered. International financial institutions can demonstrate and influence inclusion of gender aspects as best practice for the prefeasibility study.

After the prefeasibility study is complete, a more detailed feasibility study is conducted. A key highlight is technical due diligence, in which refinement or further development of the project's design and technical specifications, contributing to gender benefits, can be proposed and examined.

Certain sectors and infrastructure provide greater opportunity to incorporate gender-inclusive design features. To develop the most effective and relevant design or service features of infrastructure, collection and analysis of sex-disaggregated data are imperative. In most cases, projects can use past studies and research as a more cost-effective approach to fill data gaps and to inform project interventions from a gender perspective. However, in the absence of preexisting data, reliance on primary data collection is also important. In using either and/or both types of data sources, project teams can consider whether the collected data is sex disaggregated (i.e., if women and men have participated equally in providing insights and informing the project) and whether the data is enough to identify trends and inform analysis. Table 2 lists some of the available tools and data sources.

Table 2: Sample Tools and Data Sources

Primary Sources
Surveys
Focus group discussions (with women in communities)
Consultations (government, women's groups, associations, community groups, and others)
Interviews with key informants
Legislation and policy analysis
Secondary Sources
Census statistics
Country gender assessments or gender analysis, gender briefs, or sector analysis conducted by other development partners
Project reports, e.g., project completion reports and extended annual review reports of related sector projects in the resident mission of ADB
Previous impact assessments done by government or international organizations, and the country gender assessment
Surveys by nongovernment organizations and research institutions
Data by business, trade, and community associations
Studies and reports

ADB = Asian Development Bank.
Source: ADB.

This information can also possibly be gathered during the ESIA. The ESIA could be enhanced by integrating specific queries relevant to gender analyses. Any consultations (individual, stakeholder, community) should be gender-inclusive so that respondents can provide unbiased information. This is particularly important for collecting qualitative information or examining issues in detail. Consultations with women and men ensure greater support for the project within the community, while women's participation and consideration of their perspectives help to bring better and broader benefits to users.[17]

---

17   IFC. 2018. *Women and Community Engagement—Tool Suite 3: Unlocking Opportunities for Women and Business.* Washington, DC. https://documents1.worldbank.org/curated/en/653501532466173992/pdf/128789-WP-v3-IFC-Gender-Report-2018-Tool-Suite-3-Women-and-Comm-engagement-PUBLIC.pdf.

Table 3 summarizes key gender issues for consideration in a project feasibility assessment, and Box 7 presents an example of a gender-inclusive project feasibility of a school infrastructure.

Table 3: Gender Issues for Consideration in Assessing Project Feasibility

Area	Main Gender Issues and Questions
Economic analysis	Gender aspects of economic analysis can be incorporated through collection of sex-disaggregated data to analyze benefits of the project for women (direct and indirect). For example, by establishing the current ratio of users between men and women as a baseline, we can factor in the change in number of women users by integrating gender-inclusive design features of the proposed infrastructure. Based on this analysis, if an increase in the number of women users is expected, then additional benefits can be quantified and reflected in the cost–benefit comparison. Potential questions to explore may cover the following: ■ *What is the current access to services and infrastructure for men and women?* ■ *Are there specific gender design features (which could be identified in the technical due diligence) that could facilitate an increase in women's access and use of the infrastructure and/or services?* ■ *How can an increase in women users be factored into the projected economic benefits and returns from the infrastructure and/or service compared with additional costs that may be required to incorporate gender-inclusive design features?*
Financial analysis	In financial analysis, PPP projects can explore demand by women users for the product or service they offer. Such demand, as well as links and correlation between the intended number of women and men users, is analyzed and considered for the fee structure. Questions to explore may include the following: ■ *How big an increase in women users can the project expect?* ■ *How can women contribute to the expansion of the overall user base and increase cash flow?* ■ *How can affordability impact women's and men's use of product and services?* ■ *Are subsidies envisaged and/or available to ensure affordability among vulnerable groups?* ■ *What will be the net financial impact of cost increases because of gender considerations and revenue increases generated through the capturing of women users?*
Technical due diligence	During technical due diligence, technical specifications of planned infrastructure will be reviewed to see if gender needs can be addressed by optimizing certain technical details, or if new facilities or components are needed to make it gender-inclusive. ■ *Does the project have any gender-inclusive design features that can facilitate women's access, safety, and affordability of the infrastructure and/or services?* ■ *Is such design implementable? If not, could gender issues be addressed at the service level?* ■ *Will the project facilitate the narrowing down of gender gaps (e.g., women's economic participation; sexual exploitation, abuse, and harassment risks)?*
Legal due diligence	Applying a gender lens to legal due diligence could include the following aspects and considerations: ■ *Are the responsibilities of addressing genders issues reasonably allocated across project parties under the project contracts?* ■ *What are labor laws, and do they allow equal participation of women across sectors? Are there any laws that address women's entrepreneurship?* ■ *Do large and small equipment suppliers and/or construction companies have equal access to participate in a bid? Are there any monopoly-preventive provisions?*

PPP = public–private partnership.
Source: Asian Development Bank.

Box 7

Good Practice Approach: Inclusion of Gender Equality Issues in Project Feasibility Studies—Example of a School Infrastructure Project

Information gathering:

(i) Assess gender and other social inequality issues by collecting data and information through secondary sources (e.g., the education sector plan and the Asian Development Bank's country partnership strategy or country gender assessment) to identify specific gender gaps in the education sector and schooling.

(ii) Interview women during stakeholder consultations as part of the environmental and social impact assessment, and ensure a separate list or document is kept to highlight needs/priorities/challenges.

Analysis of findings:

(i) Overall parity may exist in enrollment, but there could be issues with (a) higher dropout levels among girls because of access to schools, which can be solved by constructing new schools in high-demand areas if there are safe and accessible transport options; and (b) retention, which may relate more to the actual design aspects of the school.

(ii) Other inclusion issues, especially for children with special education needs or disability issues, can be quite complex, as excluded children face additional barriers to accessing schools. This could be further explored in assessments.

Potential entry points for improving inclusiveness and gender responsiveness:

(i) Provide separate male and female toilets and changing rooms, supported with proper and adequate signage.

(ii) Provide health-related awareness raising and proper water and sanitation practices, particularly focusing on girls' needs that can help reduce absenteeism in both adolescent girls and (women) teachers.

(iii) Ensure that facility management company has an adequate percentage of women as facility caretakers.

(iv) Promote a safe and protective school environment and improve institutional safety through a code of conduct and trainings for the facility management staff, in line with gender-sensitive child-friendly practices, awareness raising on sexual harassment, violence, bullying, and language and/or behavior that can be abusive or offensive for children.

(v) Address safety, as parking and drop-off areas can be a point of concern for safety.

(vi) Address special-needs children and ensure disability inclusion, and consider assistive technologies and measures (e.g., install ramps, speakers, proper signage).

Source: Authors.

(ii)   Defining and confirming scope and structure of contracts

When different types of project contracts are considered, the final contract modality and scope are determined based on the outcomes of the due diligence. In most cases, no direct impact to gender equality can be observed from different contractual structures. However, there could be instances where feasibility studies may identify key gender issues stemming from the choice of a specific contractual structure. For example, if, in a railway project, the train system is separated from management of the rail and other infrastructure services, as opposed to integrated operations, some gender-inclusive features may fall through the cracks because of the separation of responsibilities. It is therefore important to identify and define key responsibilities of gender-inclusive features or actions under different contractual modalities, and to ensure that the responsibilities are adequately allocated to each party. Consideration may also need to be given to allocating specific resources for gender actions required to prevent risks, increase usage, and ensure participation of women.

(iii)   Developing technical requirements and refining cost estimates

Detailed specifications for architecture, construction methods, and/or a reference design (as a basis of bidders' preparation for their technical proposals) are completed at this stage. The design and/or architecture of infrastructure and the services it provides should consider gender needs and benefits and integrate technical specifications to operationalize these features. The key question is to what extent the project has gender-inclusive design features that can facilitate women's access, safety, and affordability of the infrastructure and its services. Based on these considerations, overall cost estimates may need to be revised. However, both increases in costs and increases in economic benefits stemming from the inclusion of women should be analyzed to ensure unbiased views. A sample gender gap examination is presented in Table 4.

Table 4: Sample Examination of Gender Gaps for a Public Transport System

Understanding Needs and Priorities	Identifying Gendered Differences	Identifying Gender Actions
Understanding what types of transport women and men use and for what purpose	This will depend on the different roles that men and women play. Are passengers using transport to go from home to the office at peak hours? Or are they trip-chaining to perform multiple tasks such as dropping children off at school, shopping for household items at multiple places, and returning home? Based on the purpose, they may use the bus system, or need to use a combination of bus, moto-taxi, and mass rapid transit.	Offer off-peak hour discount prices to enable women to carry out multiple tasks during the day. Offer trip-chaining tickets that allow multiple stops and trips. Ensure better bus routes, stops, and connectivity to multiple destinations.

continued on next page

Table 4 *continued*

Understanding Needs and Priorities	Identifying Gendered Differences	Identifying Gender Actions
Understanding the reasons why women and men may not choose to use public transport system	There could be some similarities for men and women, such as schedules being unreliable or the buses or trains being old and facing frequent breakdowns. There could be some issues that impact women more, such as no priority seating for pregnant women or women with small children; entrances and aisles that are too narrow to fit a baby carriage; inadequate safety measures like a lack of handrails; no escalators in train stations, making them difficult to navigate with bags; or inadequate sanitation facilities at train stations.	Provide clearly marked priority seating for pregnant women, women with children, and older people. Design entrances to buses and trains with ramps and safety rails. Design broader walkways and aisles in trains and buses to fit baby carriages. Ensure that toilets in train stations have clean running water as well as a cleaner or attendant to maintain the toilets.
Understanding safety concerns of women and men, such as lighting, design and location of the stations, and the setting up of safe zones	There could be similar concerns for both men and women, for instance if bus drivers drive dangerously. Differences can be observed with respect to women being subjected to harassment or attacks.	Provide an easily accessible complaint mechanism in case of a safety incident. Display posters about zero tolerance on sexual harassment and information about support hotlines. Have trained public transport staff on hand to deal with cases of sexual harassment and attacks. Appoint and make safety officers visible. Employ more women as part of the frontline staff.

Source: Asian Development Bank

(iv)   Developing and finalizing contractual structure (including payment mechanism)

At this stage, the final contractual structure is defined to confirm all key commercial terms prior to the drafting of contracts. Optimal risk allocation is examined and firmed up, and the economic analysis may be revisited, as the final contract structure may have implications for revenue forecasts (particularly for projects that rely on user fees). Gender-related provisions that have been identified through the preceding assessments can be considered in final contractual arrangements. However, allocation of undertakings, risks, and obligations related to gender mainstreaming should be determined carefully to realize the anticipated outcomes.

For example, if specific subsidies for fees of women users are considered for a transport project, provision of subsidies would be the government's responsibility (and not the private partner's). However, the private partner should be responsible for ensuring that subsidies are made available to a specific target (i.e., women users) to actualize the anticipated gender impacts. To ensure compliance with the requirements, PPP contracts can include penalties or, in some cases, incentives in the form of bonuses for the private sector. Formulation of gender-related actions as indicators that are measurable (often as key performance indicators) can also contribute to monitoring and measuring of the contractual obligations. These approaches for PPP contracts can increase accountability of private sector, enforce responsibility toward achievement of gender equality results, and allow better management of gender-related risks.

(v)   **Defining qualification criteria, and structuring and drafting the request for qualification**

Qualification is a condition that must be met by a party to participate in the bid on concession. In order to screen and short-list interested parties, requests for proposal set minimum requirements for the capability of bid participants. This stage could consider whether experiences of gender mainstreaming can be a qualification criterion. However, it requires careful deliberation, as it may end up reducing the number of companies and/or consortiums able to participate in the bid, which may reduce the likelihood of the project's success.

Options for bid documents are summarized in Box 8. These options can be considered based on country context (if there are specific laws and requirements by the DMC) and a sector context (if it is a sector that could accelerate gender equality goals).

Box 8

Gender Considerations and Criteria for Bidding Qualification

(i)   Adherence to inclusion or diversity of its own company (supplier) and its subcontractors.

(ii)   Demonstrated previous experience of gender-inclusive approaches, policies, or practices.

(iii) Gender-sensitive policies or code of conduct, e.g., how to address harassment or violence, and its mechanism of implementation.

Source: Asian Development Bank.

(vi)   **Defining proposal requirements and evaluation criteria, and structuring and drafting the request for proposal**

At this stage, formal requirements for bid submission are defined. These include what should be presented and in what form, to allow for evaluation. This is also when the evaluation criteria will be established; the winning bidder is selected and the concession is awarded based on these criteria. During the definition of bid requirements and evaluation criteria while drafting the requests for proposal, gender considerations may be applied if the DMC has any policies that require integrating minimum standards for gender equality. Box 9 presents an example in Vanuatu of a project bidding document incorporating gender provisions.

Certain gender considerations can be taken into account when PPP contracts are drafted, which the private company would be required to fulfill. These should be aligned with the host country's gender policies and strategies. The key performance indicator on gender aspects could include all and/or some of the provisions in Table 5 that would oblige the private partner.

Box 9

Good Practice Approach: Gender in Bidding Document—Vanuatu's Aviation Investment Project by the World Bank

Vanuatu has some of the highest prevalence of gender-based violence (GBV) in the world. The project team preparing the Vanuatu Aviation Investment Project incorporated mechanisms that reduced the risks of GBV. The team included provisions in bidding documents for runway civil works that mandate the contractor to take responsibility for implementation, enforcement, and monitoring of a code of conduct covering GBV. The project established codes of conduct and an action plan to prevent GBV as well as violence against children. Through the contractor, the project also established a working relationship with a local organization to manage referrals and service provisions for victims of violence.

Sources: World Bank Group. 2019. *Gender Equality, Infrastructure and PPPs*. Washington, DC. https://ppp.worldbank.org/public-private-partnership/sites/ppp.worldbank.org/files/2020-09/Gender-and-PPPs_Report_interactive.pdf. The project details can be found here: World Bank. Vanuatu Aviation Investment Project. https://projects.worldbank.org/en/projects-operations/project-detail/P154149?lang=en&tab=overview.

Table 5: Menu of Options to Include Gender Considerations in Public–Private Partnership Contracts

Gender Provision	Indicators (Examples)
Ensure proper allocation of responsibilities of gender actions	There are distinct roles expected for the public and the private sectors. For example, it is the grantor's responsibility to monitor any changes and/or amendments to gender-related laws and policies, and to notify the concessionaire of such changes. In the meantime, it is the concessionaire's responsibility to undertake key actions required by relevant laws. These different roles need to be clearly defined and provided in project contracts.
Develop a gender-sensitive stakeholder engagement plan that demonstrates the engagement of men and women, including how information related to the project is disclosed and how grievance mechanisms are established and made accessible to all	Stakeholder and community engagement plan outlining specific measures to engage women is developed. Gender-differentiated priorities, needs, and challenges are identified and included in the environmental and social impact assessment, resettlement plans, and/or other assessments. Information on how the grievance redress mechanism receives and facilitates resolution of concerns raised by women and men about the private parties' performance is shared in periodic reports.

continued on next page

Table 5 *continued*

Gender Provision	Indicators (Examples)
Promote women's employment	Minimum target of women employed during the project cycle is established (based on data about existing participation of women in the sector or area). Internship opportunities to bring more women into the sector is developed (in cases where there may not be enough women to take up new employment opportunities). Statistics and sex-disaggregated data about the number of women employed are shared in periodic reports.
Prevent and address sexual exploitation, abuse, and harassment within the company as well as project sites	Code of conduct and/or policy to prevent and address sexual exploitation, abuse, and harassment in the workplace and project site are in place and/or developed. Reference to awareness raising on women's safety and prevention of sexual exploitation, abuse, and harassment are shared in periodic reports.
Develop and/or adopt gender-inclusive workplace practices	Gender-inclusive workplace policies are introduced (e.g., gender-inclusive human resource policy focusing on retention, skills development, mentorship, and career advancement of women; equal employment opportunities policy; parental leave policy; and special provisions for women posted in field offices and/or remote locations). Practices to support a gender-inclusive workplace are introduced (e.g., awareness raising on safe workplace practices; zero-tolerance for sexual exploitation, abuse, and harassment; private and safe facilities for women and men; separate toilet facilities for women and men; childcare support that enables women to engage in employment opportunities; provision of creche services in the workplace; and provision of flexible work shifts).
Address gender-differentiated needs for infrastructure and services	Information about how women's specific needs for access, safety, and affordability have been taken into account in the delivery of services is shared in periodic reports. Sex-disaggregated data about the users of the infrastructure and service are collected and shared periodically in reports.

Source: Asian Development Bank.

(vii) Interacting during the pre-tender period by sharing information with bidders through a data room

In addition to tender documents, there may be reference information that should be provided to bid participants. Such information is usually provided through a data room. At this stage, as part of the bidding documents and package, sex-disaggregated data and information (as collected by the government or through a feasibility study) required for bid participants to address key gender-inclusive requirements and to design their proposal should be provided in the data room.

(viii) Tendering and contracting

At this stage, the preferred bidder has been selected and final negotiations take place to clarify elements of the proposal or contract. It is important to ensure that specific gender provisions included in the request for proposal and communicated to all bidders are also included in the final contract.

Box 10 presents an example of a health-care PPP project in Uzbekistan integrating gender measures for the private sector.

Box 10

Good Practice Approach: Processes in Promoting Gender Equality for the Private Sector in a Public–Private Partnership Project

NephroPlus Dialysis Public–Private Partnership Project in Uzbekistan

The project involves the construction of infrastructure for dialysis centers in Uzbekistan. The following gender measures have been identified as part of the project's development performance indicators to be integrated into the private sector company operations:

Output 2: Increase the gender equality in the number of trained personnel

2a. Target proportion of women in the number of health personnel trained in using dialysis machines
2b. Target proportion of women in the number of health personnel trained in conducting peritoneal dialysis treatment

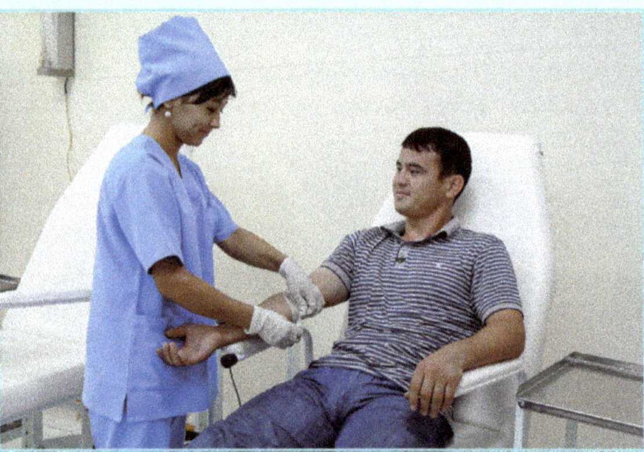

Life-saving dialysis treatment. ADB financing has supported the establishment of four dialysis centers as part of a public–private partnership (PPP) arrangement to enhance health-care service delivery in Uzbekistan. The transaction represents ADB's first financing of private health care in Uzbekistan and supports the country's first international health-care PPP (photo by ADB).

Output 3: Increase the gender responsiveness in NephroPlus workplace

3a. Increase the share of women in management positions
3b. Increase the share of women in total staffing
3c. Increase staff awareness on diversity and inclusion policies and practices, including on antisexual harassment covering both staff-to-staff relations as well as staff-to-patients relations

Source: Asian Development Bank. 2022. *FAST Report: Loan and Administration of Loan to Nephrocare Health Services Central Asia for the NephroPlus Dialysis Public–Private Partnership Project in Uzbekistan*. Gender Action Plan (accessible from the list of linked documents in Appendix 2). Manila.

Gender Actions for Downstream Assistance

⊸ KEY MESSAGES ⊸

- **Gender considerations for downstream assistance are of particular relevance for commercial investors and lenders. Monitoring is important to ensure operationalization of gender actions and to make actual positive impacts.**
- **Considerations for monitoring include the following:**
  - (i)   Collection of sex-disaggregated data,
  - (ii) Consultations with women during implementation and upon completion,
  - (iii) Updates on gender actions in the progress report, and
  - (iv) Tracking and monitoring of compliance with the contracted obligations.

Gender considerations for downstream assistance are of particular relevance for commercial investors and lenders. Finance agreements should ensure the concessionaire's undertakings to operationalize gender benefits that have been agreed with the project parties. The responsibility of the lender to monitor the concessionaire's performance to carry out such undertakings is also critical.

Once a concession has been awarded to a private partner and financial close has been achieved, PPP projects move to the development stage. Financial support is provided for construction and, post-completion, for operation and maintenance (O&M). During construction and O&M, key gender activities required under the concession agreement and/or the finance agreements, if any, must be monitored. Monitoring is important to ensure operationalization of gender actions and to make actual positive impacts.

As is common practice, progress reports on the construction activities and O&M are prepared by an independent engineer and delivered to the concessionaire. It is ideal if progress on gender actions is also included in these reports so the concessionaire is made aware of what is progressing well and what is not.

Establishing a grievance redress mechanism to inform the progress of the project is important so that women and men can voice concerns. This mechanism can also track if gender actions are not being implemented. It can likewise increase overall accountability and performance.

Considerations for monitoring include the following:

- Collecting sex-disaggregated data,
- Consulting women during implementation and upon completion,
- Including updates on gender actions in the progress report, and
- Tracking and monitoring of compliance with the contracted obligations.

3.5 Summary of the Key Questions for the Public–Private Partnership Project Cycle

◦ **KEY MESSAGE** ◦

- **There are several gender considerations along the PPP development cycle that practitioners can consider in line with core approaches for gender mainstreaming, recommended actions, and good practice examples:**
  - (i) Identify whether a project has potential to promote gender equality and avoid gender risks from the earliest stage;
  - (ii) Identify gender differences in needs and constraints as well as opportunities through gender analysis;
  - (iii) Design infrastructure or the services it provides to serve women and men equally, or to provide additional benefits to women; and
  - (iv) Monitor progress of agreed gender actions throughout project implementation.

Table 6 provides a summary of key questions to address during the project cycle; whereas, the gender considerations under the three main pillars of ADB's PPP operations are presented in Figure 6.

Table 6: Checklist—Summary of the Key Questions for the Public-Private Partnership Project Cycle

Upstream	Midstream	Downstream
Awareness Raising, Capacity Development, Policy and Institutional Reform	Project Preparation (Transaction Advisory)	Project Financing
✓ Has awareness raising of the government on gender equality taken place?	✓ Has the project identified any gender benefits or risks?	✓ Are monitoring mechanisms and resources in place to track progress on the borrowers' gender undertakings?
✓ Has knowledge sharing on benefits of integration of gender in infrastructure been carried out for government?	✓ Have women's perspectives informed project design? Have their needs related to the project been identified?	✓ Are women consulted and included in the monitoring?
✓ To what extent can existing legal frameworks promote gender equality?	✓ Has bidders' ability to manage gender risks been considered for identifying the right partner?	✓ Are data collected and analyzed from a gender perspective to learn the outcomes of the project for women and men?
✓ Does the PPP legal framework have gender-related provisions?	✓ Are gender actions and/or indicators for infrastructure design and service developed?	
✓ Does the new PPP unit have the capacity, knowledge, and mechanisms in place to promote gender equality in PPP projects?	✓ Are gender provisions included in PPP contracts?	

PPP = public–private partnership.
Source: Asian Development Bank.

Figure 6: Gender Considerations at a Glance

Upstream	**Midstream**	**Downstream**

Raise awareness of the relevance of gender equality to public–private partnerships

Build government capacity to promote gender equality

Advocate for the benefits of considering gender for infrastructure projects

Scope out existing gender policies and gender-sensitive frameworks

Integrate gender-related regulations into public–private partnerships frameworks

Conduct initial gender assessment at project definition

Define or confirm scope and structure of contracts for gender

Examine gender as part of development of technical requirements

Develop and finalize contractual structure for gender actions or indicators

Define qualification criteria, or draft Request for Quotation with gender considerations

Define proposal requirement and evaluation criteria, or draft Request for Proposal

Communicate gender considerations in tendering and contracting

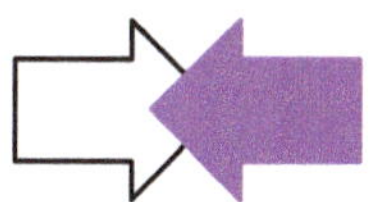

Include in concession contracts concessionaire's undertakings to operationalize gender benefits that have been integrated into project design

Operationalize gender actions

Monitor gender actions

Include grievance and redress mechanism

Source: Asian Development Bank.

APPENDIXES

Appendix 1: Useful Terms and Definitions

Gender analysis is a systematic approach to study the differences in needs, conditions, participation, priorities of men and women, and the variable impact of development on men and women. It uses sex-disaggregated quantitative and qualitative data to understand men's and women's different roles, responsibilities, decision-making power, incentives, and access to productive resources, etc. Gender analysis includes contextual analysis of the socioeconomic, legal, and political environment as they affect understanding of gender-based roles and constraints in society.
Source: European Institute for Gender Equality. Gender Analysis. https://eige.europa.eu/gender-mainstreaming/tools-methods/gender-analysis?language_content_entity=en.

Gender blind refers to the failure to realize that there are different gender roles, needs, or responsibilities of men, women, boys, and girls, as well as failure to recognize that policies, programs, and projects can have differentiated impact.
Source: United Nations Entity for Gender Equality and the Empowerment of Women (UN Women). UN Women Training Centre eLearning Campus. Gender Equality Glossary. https://trainingcentre.unwomen.org/mod/glossary/view.php?id=36&mode=letter&hook=G&sortkey=&sortorder=.

Gender equality means that men and women have equal opportunities, rights, and responsibilities. It does not mean that women and men have to become the same but that their rights, responsibilities, and opportunities should not depend on whether born male or female. Gender equality is a human rights issue as well as a condition for people-centered development.
Source: European Institute for Gender Equality. Glossary and Thesaurus. https://eige.europa.eu/publications-resources/thesaurus/terms/1059.

Gender mainstreaming is an approach for integration of gender issues. It is a process of assessing the implications for women and men of any planned action, including legislation, policies, or programs, in all areas and at all levels. It is a way to make both women's and men's concerns and experiences an integral dimension of the design, implementation, monitoring, and evaluation of policies and programs in all political, economic, and societal spheres so that women and men benefit equally; and inequality is not perpetuated. The ultimate goal is to achieve gender equality.
Source: United Nations Entity for Gender Equality and the Empowerment of Women (UN Women). UN Women Training Centre eLearning Campus. Gender Equality Glossary. https://trainingcentre.unwomen.org/mod/glossary/view.php?id=36&mode=letter&hook=G&sortkey=&sortorder=.

Gender-neutral refers to a "policy, programme, or situation that has no differential positive or negative impact in terms of gender relations or equality between women and men."

"The term 'gender-neutral' means that something is not associated with either women or men. It may refer to various aspects such as concepts or style of language. However, what is often perceived to be gender-neutral, including in areas of statistics or dissemination of data collected in reference to a population, often reflects gender blindness in practice (a failure to recognize gender specificities)."
Source: European Institute for Gender Equality. Glossary and Thesaurus. https://eige.europa.eu/publications-resources/thesaurus/terms/1321.

Gender-sensitive refers to "policies and programmes that take into account the particularities pertaining to the lives of both women and men, while aiming to eliminate inequalities and promote gender equality, including an equal distribution of resources, therefore addressing and taking into account the gender dimension."
Source: European Institute for Gender Equality. Glossary and Thesaurus. https://eige.europa.eu/publications-resources/thesaurus/terms/1324.

Appendix 2: Terms of Reference for a Gender Specialist

Purpose: To support the process of gender mainstreaming in public–private partnership (PPP) projects.

The gender specialist is expected to carry out the following tasks:

- Provide gender expertise during the PPP project screening

- Perform review and screening of laws, policies, and the overall enabling environment relevant for the PPP project

- Identify the capacity-building needs on gender equality of stakeholders and primarily the government and the private sector of the PPP project

- Provide capacity building on gender equality, including the relevance of gender equality issues to the sector or project, principles of gender mainstreaming, and monitoring of gender equality results

- Collect data from existing sources and carry out further research to inform the PPP project with gender analysis

- Gender mainstream the PPP project feasibility studies by providing gender expertise (e.g., review and provide inputs to the methodology, questionnaires)

- Participate in or carry out stakeholder consultations by adopting gender-inclusive stakeholder consultations and communications

- Carry out gender analysis of the key issues relevant for the PPP project

- Provide support in assessing the risks and opportunities of the PPP project for promoting gender equality as well as help identify the potential impacts on women and men

- Propose gender considerations for the PPP project by identifying specific actions and defining targets, including providing advice on formulation of specific gender considerations for PPPs

- Advise on monitoring of project gender equality results

- Perform other tasks that inform the project definition, preparation, and overall gender mainstreaming of the PPP project

Appendix 3: Summary of Gender Entry Points for Public–Private Partnership Projects by Sector

ENERGY			
Gender Design Features and Actions (What?)	Relevance to the Project	Approaches for PPP Projects (How?)	Alignment with Operational Priority 2 Strategic Priorities and Gender Tag
Project Planning Stage			
Ensure PPP project considers women's and men's needs and constraints for accessing energy infrastructure and/or services	Inclusive and evidence-based planning	Collect primary and/or secondary data to inform project planning from a gender perspective Identify and document needs and constraints of women as users of energy infrastructure and services related to the project, including for accessibility, affordability, capacity building, and other related issues Plan energy infrastructure addressing constraints for women	2.3: Gender equality in decision-making and leadership enhanced
Project Implementation Stage			
Address gender in affordability of services	Affordability to various groups of energy and services	Implement differentiated pricing schemes needed to ensure low-income women are able to maintain access to an affordable electricity supply Implement subsidized payment practices	2.1: Women's economic empowerment increased 2.4: Women's time poverty and drudgery reduced

continued on next page

Appendix 3 *continued*

ENERGY

Gender Design Features and Actions (What?)	Relevance to the Project	Approaches for PPP Projects (How?)	Alignment with Operational Priority 2 Strategic Priorities and Gender Tag
Focus on the services that meet the needs of communities, including women	Better informed services	Invest in streetlights to ensure safety for women and girls, who are particularly vulnerable Provide electrification for facilities such as hospitals and schools for local communities of the targeted area Engage in awareness raising of women in power generation and power-saving measures as key users and managers of energy in households Enhance women's participation in community-managed distribution systems (e.g., through capacity building or quotas) Establish mobile sales points to cater to women (i.e., arrange them at places and times that are easily accessible to women) Establish a number and/or proportion for increasing women's employment in the energy sector or company Establish a number and/or proportion for increasing women employees hired for management roles	2.4: Women's time poverty and drudgery reduced

continued on next page

Appendix 3 *continued*

ENERGY

Gender Design Features and Actions (What?)	Relevance to the Project	Approaches for PPP Projects (How?)	Alignment with Operational Priority 2 Strategic Priorities and Gender Tag
Promote women's employment	Diversified workforce	Establish a number and/or proportion for increasing women employees in technical roles Involve women (by setting a number and/or proportion) as maintenance and meter reader agents Increase the number of women customer service representatives having a direct interface with women and households headed by women Establish a number and/or proportion for increasing women interns in technical roles Develop and implement an equal opportunity policy Adopt a gender inclusion policy for energy companies, particularly focusing on hiring, retention, and promotion of women staff Adopt an antisexual harassment policy Train staff (number or percentage) annually on the company's antisexual harassment policy	2.1: Women's economic empowerment increased 2.2: Gender equality in human development enhanced 2.3: Gender equality in decision-making and leadership enhanced
Women's economic empowerment	New opportunities and empowerment of women	Offer livelihood development training or opportunities to women of the targeted communities (number of women participants)	2.1: Women's economic empowerment increased

continued on next page

Appendix 3 *continued*

HEALTH

Gender Design Features and Actions (What?)	Relevance to the Project	Approaches for PPP Projects (How?)	Alignment with Operational Priority 2 Strategic Priorities and Gender Tag
Project Planning Stage			
Gender differences in accessibility to services	Inclusive and evidence-based planning	Identify women's and men's needs in the access to services	2.3: Gender equality in decision-making and leadership enhanced
Gender differences in affordability of services		Collect primary and/or secondary data to inform the project	
		Identify gender differences in affordability of services (various levels)	
Project Implementation Stage			
Address gender equality needs in the project, in particular the offer of services and prices	Improved access to and affordability of infrastructure and services	Define services and prices by considering the different needs and constraints of women	2.4: Women's time poverty and drudgery reduced 2.5: Women's resilience to external shocks strengthened
Capacity building	Enhancing skills	Capacity building to support women's employment and women's career advancement in the project or sector	2.2: Gender equality in human development enhanced
Employment and workplace practices	Increasing economic opportunities	Establish number and/or proportion for women's employment in private company or sector Create safe workplace for women (antisexual harassment mechanism) or provide women-friendly workplaces	2.1: Women's economic empowerment increased 2.5: Women's resilience to external shocks strengthened
Specific sexual and reproductive needs	Better response and readiness	Raise awareness on specific issues for women (e.g., reproductive health) Raise awareness of medical staff on gender-based violence to be able to recognize victims of violence	2.5: Women's resilience to external shocks strengthened

continued on next page

Appendix 3 *continued*

EDUCATION

Gender Design Features and Actions (What?)	Relevance to the Project	Approaches for PPP Projects (How?)	Alignment with Operational Priority 2 Strategic Priorities and Gender Tag
Project Preparation Stage			
Identify gender issues and differences	Inclusive and evidence-based planning	Gender data collection, gender-inclusive consultations, and analysis to identify and document the needs of women and men, and girls and boys, in in the education sector or company related to the project	2.3: Gender equality in decision-making and leadership enhanced
Project Implementation Stage			
Infrastructure meets the needs of women and girls	Gender-inclusive infrastructure	Introduce separate male and female toilets with adequate signage; provide privacy in medical rooms for girls Introduce ramps instead of steps for easier wheelchair access	2.5: Women's resilience to external shocks strengthened
Introduce gender equality in facility management	Gender-inclusive management	Employ women as facility caretakers (e.g., managers, security personnel, cleaners)	2.1: Women's economic empowerment increased
Promote safe environment	Establish inclusive practices and improved attendance	Provide training to the facility management in line with gender-sensitive child-friendly practices	2.2: Gender equality in human development enhanced
		Conduct awareness raising on areas such as violence and sexual harassment against women and girls, bullying, and abusive behavior for facility management personnel	2.5: Women's resilience to external shocks strengthened
Awareness raising	Improved services	Target girls and boys in the evacuation awareness raising based on any possible differing needs	2.5: Women's resilience to external shocks strengthened
		Awareness raising on health-related practices, particularly focusing on girls' needs and reducing absenteeism in both adolescent girls and (women) teachers	2.2: Gender equality in human development enhanced

continued on next page

Appendix 3 *continued*

INFORMATION AND COMMUNICATION TECHNOLOGY

Gender Design Features and Actions (What?)	Relevance to the Project	Approaches for PPP Projects (How?)	Alignment with Operational Priority 2 Strategic Priorities and Gender Tag
Project Planning Stage			
PPP project considers needs and constraints for women and men	Inclusive and evidence-based planning	Gender data collection and analysis to identify and documents needs of women and men in the ICT sector or company related to the project	2.3: Gender equality in decision-making and leadership enhanced
Project Implementation Stage			
Technology choice	Tailored approaches	Affordable services for women Offer user-friendly technology, particularly in the context of relatively low literacy levels Offer pricing for services that ensures affordability for women	2.5: Women's resilience to external shocks strengthened
Capacity building for women	Building technical capacity	Extend opportunities for capacity building to women as well as men Provide mechanisms to encourage women to enter ICT fields (e.g., through organization of campaigns, role models, training of students) Carry out campaigns in the communities that target young women to spur their interest in the sector	2.2: Gender equality in human development enhanced
Gender-inclusive initiatives to target more women in ICT	Diversifying opportunities	Target women in internship opportunities Company-sponsored or initiated mentorship and leadership training seminars for women in the ICT sector	2.2: Gender equality in human development enhanced

continued on next page

Appendix 3 *continued*

INFORMATION AND COMMUNICATION TECHNOLOGY

Gender Design Features and Actions (What?)	Relevance to the Project	Approaches for PPP Projects (How?)	Alignment with Operational Priority 2 Strategic Priorities and Gender Tag
Gender mainstreaming policies and practices within a company	Equal opportunities	Adopt a gender equality policy, an equal opportunities policy, and related policies within a company to increase women's employment Set targets for promoting equality among newly hired staff within a company	2.1: Women's economic empowerment increased

ICT = information and communication technology, PPP = public–private partnership.
Source: Asian Development Bank.

Appendix 4: Selected Crosscutting Gender Considerations for Public–Private Partnerships and Business Cases

Crosscutting Gender Actions, Indicators, and Business Case	
Gender Actions	**Illustrative Indicators**

Women's Employment

- Employ women in project-related jobs
- Create new employment opportunities for women

- Percentage of women employed at different phases of the public–private partnership project as appropriate[a]
- Number and share of women in the new jobs created

The Business Case

Supporting women's economic empowerment is a key opportunity area for delivering gender impact through public–private partnership projects. Addressing women's economic empowerment can be used as leverage to create positive changes for gender equality and broader benefits for women, communities, and countries.[b] More and more companies across Asia and the Pacific acknowledge the benefits of supporting women's economic inclusion and supporting women-owned businesses. Studies demonstrate that promoting gender equality and women's higher participation in companies and economies increases profitability and efficiency, and brings long-term sustainability.[c] Studies also show that the equal involvement of women in the workplace contributes to returns on investment for businesses and boosts women's economic empowerment, making them more likely to invest their money back into their families through spending on children's health and education, which also generates sustainable and positive development outcomes.

Women's Participation, Voice, and Leadership

- Ensure women's participation at all levels

- Number and percentage of women participants in consultations
- Number and percentage of women's participation in decision-making
- Number and percentage of women's participation in trainings, campaigns, and similar initiatives
- Number and percentage of women in decision-making and leadership positions

The Business Case

Including women as users, consumers, employees, and decision-makers (e.g., on boards) is important to make them part of the processes and decisions. Because of cultural attitudes, social norms, responsibilities, and direct or indirect constraints, women may be omitted from important processes (decision-making, capacity building, etc.) that may affect their lives in the future. There is also evidence that shows the positive outcomes resulting from women's inclusion across the private sector. Gender diversity in companies brings a mix of different perspectives, talents, and skills.[d] Evidence shows that businesses with gender-diverse and inclusive boards outperform those with no women in terms of share price performance, especially during times of crisis or instability; businesses with more gender diversity better recruit and retain top talent and help make them more resilient and resourceful.[e] Indeed, women's inclusion at all levels in private sector companies is recognized as a positive practice.[f]

continued on next page

Crosscutting Gender Actions, Indicators, and Business Case

Gender Actions	Illustrative Indicators

Gender-Inclusive Workplace Policies

■ Adopt gender-inclusive workplace policies

Examples of gender-inclusive policies are
- Gender equality policy
- Gender-inclusive human resources policy (focusing on aspects including retention, skills development, and career advancement)
- Equal employment opportunities policy
- Leave policy (e.g., parental and family)
- Salary and benefits policy
- Preventing sexual exploitation and harassment policy
- Antidiscrimination policy

The Business Case

Gender-inclusive workplace policies are the foundation for more equal outcomes for women and men as well as for organizations. Gender-inclusive policies that take into account how to improve policies (and practices) for women and men facilitates improvement of an organization's business performance, helps companies meet their bottom line by increasing employee satisfaction, reduces employee turnover, and drives productivity.[g]

Effective workplace policies are important from an economic inclusion perspective, because they offer the opportunity to address the issues that particularly face women. These include things like the worldwide gender pay gap, and indirect or direct discrimination at the hiring stage or in the workplace. Studies show that gender-inclusive policies—particularly those focusing on inclusive recruitment, training, and programs that improve work–life balance for parents and/or health outcomes—have helped companies (i) increase the pool of job candidates at various levels, including for entry-level jobs and board positions; and (ii) become an employer of choice.[h]

Gender-Inclusive Workplace Practices, Occupation, and Safety

■ Create and adopt gender-inclusive workplace practices

- Code of conduct preventing gender-based violence and/or sexual exploitation, abuse, and harassment adopted
- Awareness raised on safe workplace practices
- Separate, private, and safe facilities for women and men
- Elder care and childcare-focused practices

The Business Case

Adopting gender-inclusive workplace practices helps eliminate gender concerns and helps companies create an environment that is inclusive, safe, and diverse.[i] Workplace harassment affects women regardless of age, background, income, location, or social status; avoiding discriminatory practices is the key to eliminating the problem. The economic costs (which reflect the human and social costs) to the global economy of discriminatory social institutions and violence against women are estimated to be nearly $12 trillion annually.[c]

continued on next page

Appendix 4 *continued*

Crosscutting Gender Actions, Indicators, and Business Case

Gender Actions	Illustrative Indicators

Equal Access to Services

- Address gender-differentiated needs for services of individuals (e.g., access, affordability, safety) for equal access to services
- Address gender-differentiated needs of households

- Women's and men's needs for accessing services addressed
- Women's and men's needs for affordability of services addressed
- Women's and men's needs for safety in accessing the services addressed
- Number of groups using services (e.g., women, men, households, disadvantaged households)

The Business Case

Examples across projects show the importance of consideration of needs of women and men (women and men from various backgrounds, households, older people, etc.) in project design. While their perspectives may influence the project, they may also lead to better results and outcomes that are important for the effective use of the offered service(s).

Consideration of gender-differentiated needs is not necessarily costly to implement. Sometimes, companies may be doing it anyway without necessarily acknowledging or tracking the progress, or they may not apply a gender lens to planning in a conscious manner. Examples include a transport project that is considering building infrastructure, including sanitary facilities and bus stops. From a gender perspective, consideration of the needs of women and men might lead to actions such as designing separate sanitary facilities; installing proper lighting at bus stops to prevent harassment; and installing security cameras, information boards, and related services to inform passengers of safety measures and make them feel safe while accessing and using the service. In this case, most of these elements are not necessarily related to high project costs. However, knowing who the beneficiaries are and how gender sensitivity measures can be applied can make a tremendous difference on the equal use of the infrastructure and/or service.

New Skills and Capacity Building

- Make women part of the capacity-building activities

- Gender-sensitization training conducted
- Follow-up actions of the gender training
- Number and type of trainings targeting women
- New skills developed by women

The Business Case

Investing in skills development is a foundation of progress across sectors. However, despite the significant advancement in skills development, education, and capacity building, women and girls still face barriers and discrimination that prevent them from thriving in a number of areas and fields.[j] Skills development is especially important for women's advancement into leadership roles, which can positively impact the public and private sectors. In addition, it can promote women's positive contributions to sectors where women's participation is not high (e.g., transport, engineering, information and communication technology, and other technical sectors and jobs). Ensuring that skills development approaches are more gender-inclusive is doable and can bring practical benefits to women and communities.[k]

It is equally important to increase capacity on gender-sensitive approaches in organizations and companies for positive outcomes. There are many resources available online and offline to inform stakeholders on gender equality and inclusion policies and practices.

continued on next page

Appendix 4 *continued*

Crosscutting Gender Actions, Indicators, and Business Case

Gender Actions	Illustrative Indicators

[a]   Particularly in the sectors where women are not represented, e.g., infrastructure.

[b]   Women Deliver. 2019. *Policy Brief: Boost Women's Economic Empowerment—Facts, Solutions, Case Studies, and Calls to Action.* New York. https://womendeliver.org/wp-content/uploads/2017/09/2019-7-D4G_Brief_Economic.pdf.

[c]   United Nations Entity for Gender Equality and the Empowerment of Women (UN Women). 2018. Facts and Figures: Economic Empowerment—Benefits of Economic Empowerment. https://www.unwomen.org/en/what-we-do/economic-empowerment/facts-and-figures.

[d]   Y. Argüden. 2010. Diversity at the Head Table: Bringing Complementary Skills and Experiences to the Board. *Private Sector Opinion.* No. 19. Washington, DC: International Finance Corporation (IFC). https://www.ifc.org/content/dam/ifc/doc/mgrt/ifc-pso-19-web-res.pdf.

[e]   United States Agency for International Development (USAID). 2020. *Engendering Industries: Developing a Business Case for Gender Equality.* Washington, DC. https://www.usaid.gov/sites/default/files/2022-05/USAID-Engendering-Industries-Guide-Business-Case.pdf.

[f]   V. Hunt et al. 2018. *Delivering through Diversity.* McKinsey and Company. https://www.mckinsey.com/business-functions/people-and-organizational-performance/our-insights/delivering-through-diversity.

[g]   USAID. 2022. *Engendering Industries: Integrating Gender into Workplace Policies.* Washington, DC. https://www.usaid.gov/sites/default/files/2022-11/2022-USAID-Engendering-Industries-Guide-Workplace-Policies.pdf.

[h]   IFC. 2013. *Investing in Women's Employment: Good for Business, Good for Development.* Washington, DC. https://documents1.worldbank.org/curated/en/484201468163444954/pdf/826360WP0Inves00Box379867B00PUBLIC0.pdf.

[i]   International Labour Organization. 2009. *Providing Safe and Healthy Workplaces for Both Women and Men.* Geneva. https://www.ilo.org/wcmsp5/groups/public/---dgreports/---gender/documents/publication/wcms_105060.pdf.

[j]   UN Women. Economic Empowerment and Skills Development for Young Women. https://www.unwomen.org/en/what-we-do/youth/economic-empowerment-and-skills-development-for-young-women.

[k]   More on skills training for women can be found here: K. Beegle and E. Rubiano-Matulevich. 2020. Five Ways to Make Skills Training Work for Women. *World Bank Blogs.* 22 September. https://blogs.worldbank.org/jobs/five-ways-make-skills-training-work-women.

Source: Asian Development Bank.

Appendix 5: List of Useful Resources

Gender Equality and Mainstreaming

Asian Development Bank (ADB). 2013. *Tool Kit on Gender Equality Results and Indicators*. Manila. https://www.adb.org/sites/default/files/institutional-document/34063/tool-kit-gender-equality-results-indicators_0.pdf.

European Institute for Gender Equality. Gender Mainstreaming: More Tools and Methods. https://eige.europa.eu/gender-mainstreaming/methods-tools.

United Nations Entity for Gender Equality and the Empowerment of Women (UN Women). UN Women Training Centre eLearning Campus. Gender Equality Glossary. https://trainingcentre.unwomen.org/mod/glossary/view.php?id=36&mode&hook=ALL&sortkey&sortorder&fullsearch=0&page=0.

UN Women. 2018. *Why Gender Equality Matters across All SDGs—An Excerpt of Turning Promises Into Action: Gender Equality in the 2030 Agenda for Sustainable Development*. New York. https://www.unwomen.org/sites/default/files/Headquarters/Attachments/Sections/Library/Publications/2018/SDG-report-Chapter-3-Why-gender-equality-matters-across-all-SDGs-2018-en.pdf.

World Economic Forum. 2021. *Global Gender Gap Report 2021: Insight Report*. Geneva. https://www3.weforum.org/docs/WEF_GGGR_2021.pdf.

Gender and Public–Private Partnership Tools

Caribbean Development Bank. 2018. *Integrating Gender Equality into Public–Private Sector Partnerships: Technical Guidance Note*. Saint Michael, Barbados. https://www.caribank.org/sites/default/files/publication-resources/CDB2_INTEGRATING%20GENDER%20EQUALITY%20INTO%20PUBLIC-PRIVATE%20SECTOR%20PARTNERSHIPS_final.pdf.

International Finance Corporation (IFC). 2012. *Gender Impact of Public Private Partnerships: Literature Review Synthesis Report*. Consultant's report. https://ppp.worldbank.org/public-private-partnership/sites/ppp.worldbank.org/files/documents/PIDG-IFC_Gender%20Impact%20of%20Private%20Public%20Partnerships%20in%20Infrastructure.pdf.

World Bank Group. 2019. *Gender Equality, Infrastructure and PPPs: A Primer*. Washington, DC. https://ppp.worldbank.org/public-private-partnership/sites/ppp.worldbank.org/files/2020-09/Gender-and-PPPs_Report_interactive.pdf.

Gender, Procurement, and Supply Chains

ADB and UN Women. 2021. *Gender-Responsive Procurement in Asia and the Pacific: An Opportunity for an Equitable Economic Future*. Manila. https://asiapacific.unwomen.org/sites/default/files/2022-12/GRP-Report-14-11-22.pdf.

continued on next page

Appendix 5 *continued*

BSR; Women Deliver; and Government of the Netherlands, Ministry of Foreign Affairs. 2016. *Women's Empowerment in Global Value Chains: A Framework for Business Action to Advance Women's Health, Rights, and Wellbeing.* https://www.bsr.org/reports/BSR-Report-Womens-Empowerment-Supply-Chains.pdf.

UN Women. 2017. *The Power of Procurement: How to Source from Women-Owned Businesses—Corporate Guide to Gender-Responsive Procurement.* New York. https://www.unwomen.org/sites/default/files/Headquarters/Attachments/Sections/Library/Publications/2017/The-power-of-procurement-How-to-source-from-women-owned-businesses-en.pdf.

UN Women. 2021. *Rethinking Gender-Responsive Procurement: Enabling an Ecosystem for Women's Economic Empowerment.* New York. https://www.unwomen.org/sites/default/files/Headquarters/Attachments/Sections/Library/Publications/2021/Rethinking-gender-responsive-procurement-en.pdf.

Gender and Workplace Policies and Practices

BSR. 2017. *Gender Equality in Codes of Conduct Guidance.* https://www.bsr.org/reports/BSR_Gender_Equality_in_Codes_of_Conduct_Guidance.pdf.

GenderSmart. *Justice, Equity, Diversity and Inclusion Investing Toolkit.* https://jediinvesting.com/.

Government of Australia, Workplace Gender Equality Agency. 2014. *Developing a Gender Equality Policy: Briefing Note.* Canberra. https://www.wgea.gov.au/sites/default/files/documents/Characteristics-of-a-Gender-Equality-policy.pdf.

IFC. 2013. *Investing in Women's Employment: Good for Business, Good for Development.* Washington, DC. https://documents1.worldbank.org/curated/en/484201468163444954/pdf/826360WP0Inves00Box379867B00PUBLIC0.pdf.

IFC. 2015. *Putting Gender Smart Commitments into Practice: SheWorks Year One Progress Report.* Washington, DC. https://documents1.worldbank.org/curated/en/997251468189526860/pdf/99643-WP-Box393202B-PUBLIC-disclosed-9-23-15.pdf.

International Labour Organization. 2009. *Providing Safe and Healthy Workplaces for Both Women and Men.* Geneva. https://www.ilo.org/wcmsp5/groups/public/---dgreports/---gender/documents/publication/wcms_105060.pdf.

International Labour Organization. 2020. *Empowering Women at Work: Company Policies and Practices for Gender Equality.* Geneva. https://www.ilo.org/wcmsp5/groups/public/---ed_emp/---emp_ent/---multi/documents/publication/wcms_756721.pdf.

United States Agency for International Development. 2022. *Engendering Industries: Integrating Gender into Workplace Policies.* Washington, DC. https://www.usaid.gov/engendering-industries/gender-equality-guides/policies.

continued on next page

Appendix 5 *continued*

Sector (Infrastructure)

ADB. 2012. *Gender Tool Kit: Energy—Going Beyond the Meter*. Manila. https://www.adb.org/sites/default/files/institutional-document/33650/gender-toolkit-energy_0.pdf.

ADB. 2013. *Gender Tool Kit: Transport—Maximizing the Benefits of Improved Mobility for All*. Manila. https://www.adb.org/sites/default/files/institutional-document/33901/files/gender-tool-kit-transport.pdf.

GTZ (Deutsche Gesellschaft fur Technische Zusammenarbeit). 2007. *Gender and Urban Transport: Smart and Affordable, Module 7a. Sustainable Transport: A Sourcebook for Policy-makers in Developing Cities*. Eschborn, Germany. https://ppp.worldbank.org/public-private-partnership/sites/ppp.worldbank.org/files/documents/GTZ_Gender-and-Urban-Transport_EN.pdf.

M. Jennings and C. Gaynor. 2004. *Public Private Partnerships, Infrastructure, Gender and Poverty*. Washington, DC: World Bank Institute. https://wedc-knowledge.lboro.ac.uk/docs/research/WEJR7/Guest_-_PPPI_Gender_and_Poverty_-_abridged_paper.pdf.

Organisation for Economic Co-operation and Development (OECD). Gender in Infrastructure. https://www.oecd.org/gov/infrastructure-governance/gender-in-infrastructure/.

OECD. 2021. Women in Infrastructure: Selected Stocktaking of Good Practices for Inclusion of Women in Infrastructure. *OECD Public Governance Policy Papers*. No. 07. Paris: OECD Publishing. https://doi.org/10.1787/9eab66a8-en.

World Bank. Gender and Transport. https://www.worldbank.org/en/topic/transport/publication/gender-and-transport.

World Bank. 2010. *Making Infrastructure Work for Women and Men: A Review of World Bank Group Infrastructure Projects (1995–2009)*. Washington, DC. https://ppp.worldbank.org/public-private-partnership/sites/ppp.worldbank.org/files/documents/making_infrastructure_work_women_men_a_review_wb_infra_projects1995_-_2009_2010_en.pdf.